The Brave Educator

The Brave Educator equips you with accessible and refreshingly useful tools for real conversations about race that prepare students for the world beyond the school walls. More than a toolkit, this book is a personal conversation exploring the journey from being stuck in the belief that we should already know how to lead conversations about race to learning how to actually have the conversation. It's companionship for educators, leaders, and teachers facing overwhelming daily responsibilities and searching for open-hearted support. Inside you'll find a flexible road map to help carve a path through difficult conversations in your classroom, plus question prompts, resource lists, and crucial tips to help you avoid common pitfalls. The grounded perspective and real-world examples in these pages will help you feel less alone as you move from tentative to prepared.

Krystle Cobran creates conversations about race that open the doors of connection. Her work helps us weave our stories together so we can connect more and fear less. Krystle draws on her Juris Doctor from the George Washington University Law School; her Master of Public Policy from the Thomas Jefferson Program in Public Policy at the College of William & Mary; her experience creating, developing, and teaching two conversation-driven undergraduate courses at the intersection of race and the law (Race & the Law and American Courts, Race, and Social Issues); her work as a speaker, consultant, and writer; and her love for human stories to transform seemingly impossible conversations about race into genuine dialogue that propels us forward. Her work begins with listening—to you. You can drop Krystle a note by visiting krystlecobran.com.

The Brave Educator

Honest Conversations about Navigating Race in the Classroom

Krystle Cobran

Routledge
Taylor & Francis Group

NEW YORK AND LONDON

First published 2020
by Routledge
52 Vanderbilt Avenue, New York, NY 10017

and by Routledge
2 Park Square, Milton Park, Abingdon, Oxon, OX14 4RN

*Routledge is an imprint of the Taylor & Francis Group,
an informa business*

Library of Congress Cataloging-in-Publication Data
Names: Cobran, Krystle, author.
Title: The brave educator : honest conversations about navigating race in
    the classroom / Krystle Cobran.
Description: New York : Routledge, 2020.
Identifiers: LCCN 2019014170 (print) | LCCN 2019022133 (ebook) |
    ISBN 9781138389274 (hbk) | ISBN 9781138389311 (pbk) |
    ISBN 9780429424014 (ebk)
Subjects: LCSH: Culturally relevant pedagogy. | Race—Study and
    teaching. | Classroom environment.
Classification: LCC LC1099 .C635 2020 (print) | LCC LC1099 (ebook) |
    DDC 370.117—dc23
LC record available at https://lccn.loc.gov/2019014170
LC ebook record available at https://lccn.loc.gov/2019022133

ISBN: 978-1-138-38927-4 (hbk)
ISBN: 978-1-138-38931-1 (pbk)
ISBN: 978-0-429-42401-4 (ebk)

Typeset in Palatino
by Apex CoVantage LLC

For humans doing the invisible work of educating.
You are not forgotten.

Contents

Preface

The Crucial Difference Between Conversation and Combat

Let's Forget How This Is Supposed to Go

Here's how this is supposed to go. You start talking. I keep a running checklist. My job isn't listening; it's checking to see whether the words you speak line up with my expectations about what you should say. I wait until you run out of air and need to take a breath. At that precise moment, I step in. It's my turn. Not to share. Not to connect. Not to explore the hidden places where we might discover difference and similarity, disconnection or alignment.

It's my turn to fix you. Because the running checklist is now a list of requirements I have to satisfy with every word I speak to you. Perhaps it would be more accurate to say *at* you. I must prove my point(s). Within my next breath, I must transform your thinking, your perspective, your view of the world to be more like my own, or I've failed. Since we both have lungs, I need to breathe. My gasp is your moment to speak again. I scrutinize every word you speak for evidence that I've changed you, made you a bit more like me.

I expect you to do the same.

This is what we call conversation. No connection. No genuine listening. None of the open-hearted curiosity that leads us to Make Tiny Tweaks. We aim only for massive change achieved in a moment. Forget the small moments of connection that shift things. There is only talking at each other, us trying to overpower one another.

That's not how this is going to go.

I Want to Have a Real Conversation With You

Conversation and combat aren't the same thing. Most of what we call *talking about race* is really us pelting words at, and past each other. We're having combatations. (Yes, I just made that word up.) It sounds awful—like a physical contraction. And it feels far worse.

The impact is great. When we're ignored and unsupported, learning how to talk about race in the classroom feels impossible. This loneliness hurts the heart, crushes curiosity, silences discovery, and leaves us feeling trapped between tiptoeing around the conversation or imposing our fluctuating views on our students. It's a formula for endless disconnection.

In the cauldron of education, where the pressure to perform is sky-high, resources are limited, communication happens in perpetually interrupted snippets, demands are unpredictable, and expectations are multifaceted and endless, trying to have this particular conversation together feels simultaneously necessary, overwhelming, and futile.

We're doing it anyway.

Here's How We're Going to Talk With Each Other

We're going to speak *with* each other. Not try to fix one another. We're going to share stories without ranking and comparing our pain. We'll learn together, connect, and begin to create shared understanding. We're going to put down our lists—all the expectations and obligations that weigh us down—and explore what comes in the space between knowing we need to talk about race in the classroom and leading conversations about race in the classroom that generate connection, mutual respect, and discovery.

Stuck deep inside that space is a choice utterly essential to navigating conversations about race in the classroom: giving ourselves permission to learn *how* to navigate conversations about race in the classroom. Opportunities to practice. Tools that help us turn from avoidance to interaction, from distraction to productivity. *Let's release the assumption that we're already supposed to know how to navigate conversations about race in the classroom so we can learn how to do it.* We're going to go through this process together. By having a conversation. That's what *The Brave Educator* is: a conversation about the journey of learning how to create conversations about race in the classroom.

Let's Not Pretend

I want you to feel supported.

I'm not interested in fighting you in these pages. We've only just met, but I have a feeling you're not interested in fighting me either. (All this combatation is exhausting.) I want you to feel listened to. Seen. Heard. Let's obliterate the loneliness and helplessness so many educators feel when race comes up in the classroom.

Let's share stories. I'll share some of my mistakes and stumbles. We'll talk about hard lessons I learned the hard way. I've built a flexible road map you can use to carve a path through conversations about race in your classroom, and shared crucial connection strategies to help you move from tentative to prepared.

We're going to have this conversation without the show—the show of us needing to have all the answers.

I don't have all the answers. I'm interested in having a real conversation, with you.

Introduction

Let's Start With Not Knowing Where to Start

I Thought I Had All the Answers

I had a grand plan. *I'm going to be a doctor*. My existence revolved around turning expectation into reality. I majored in microbiology and cell science at the University of Florida after years of working in a medical office, charting height, weight, and blood pressure; answering phones; and coordinating doctors' appointment schedules and patient visits. Those words sounded impressive, upped my credibility, and concealed insecurities.

Three years into my premed track and it was suddenly all too much. The burden of pretending that I had the answers and knew exactly what my future held tore at me. Appearances couldn't justify my misery. Staring my misery in the eye felt like failure. I needed time to wander so I could discover. *But you're already supposed to know. Check another box under the failure column*. Instead of exploration, I reached toward doing; earned an undergraduate degree in political science while completing a research scholarship program, and went off to the Thomas Jefferson Program in Public Policy at the College of William & Mary and William & Mary Law School as a joint law and master of public policy student. That was what logic demanded—performance.

Since one life failure was barely permissible, I doubled, quadrupled the pressure to always be the person in the room who knew exactly what she was doing, exactly where she was going, and why. Subtle and obsessive upkeep. Two years into my four-year joint-degree program, my Love proposed, and I transferred to the George Washington University Law School to complete my Juris Doctor coursework. (In collaboration, the Thomas Jefferson Program in Public Policy, William & Mary Law, and the National Center for State Courts were kind enough to award me a Bolin Fellowship and allow me to complete my master's degree from a distance with one more semester in residence.) I kept pushing, graduated, and landed a judicial clerkship in the Superior Court of the District of Columbia. I moved to two different states with my now spouse, once for his postdoctoral fellowship and again when he landed his tenure-track professor gig. The more I attempted to perform my way into proving enough-ness, the more my frustration and loneliness grew. Doing stopped working. In the middle of my now-escalated misery, I remained convinced I was supposed to have all the answers. I wasn't ready to admit that I had none.

Not Knowing Is Where Discovery Begins

Close to 30 weeks pregnant with my first child, I began building a relationship with the then-dean of the School of Public and International Affairs at the University of Georgia, Stefanie Lindquist. She knew I'd published a law journal article with the *Georgetown Journal of Modern Critical Race Perspectives* examining race in higher education admissions (aka affirmative action). Over time, our conversations evolved, and Dean Lindquist invited me to teach an undergraduate course in race and education. My entire being jumped at the chance. But there was valid cause for fear: I needed to build this course from scratch, without having the first idea about how to create a classroom environment where every student knew their voice belonged in our conversations about race.

The scale of what was before me felt massive. I needed to:

- navigate the pressure of creating a classroom environment that wasn't about shame, judgment, or me and my stuff.
- admit to myself that I was afraid to talk about race publicly.
- find, organize, and select course materials that equipped my students for productive conversation without being manipulative, deceptive, or heavy-handed.
- structure the course so that student learning came first.
- find a way to leave my personal agenda outside the four walls.
- invite students to willingly participate in the conversation (again, without manipulation or undue pressure).
- support students as they moved through the course materials and the process of learning how to have the race conversation not just with me, but *within themselves and among each other*.
- carve out space for processing, thinking, and feeling to minimize the chance that overwhelm would perpetually interfere with learning.
- be incredibly conscious of the stories and perspective each individual student brings to the race conversation.
- understand that many students question whether there's a place for them in the conversation at all.
- resist the urge to put students into boxes based on what they look or sound like.
- resist the urge to box students in based on the questions they do or do not ask.
- design classroom conversations that generate shared learning, dignity, respect, and discovery.
- protect the tenderness and courage required to engage in open classroom dialogue about race.
- acknowledge my fear.

- ◆ listen for areas where students need extra support while proactively requesting and being responsive to their feedback.
- ◆ Make Tiny Tweaks to generate consistent improvements.
- ◆ teach by asking questions, listening, and responding to the actual words students say instead of reacting to my internal assumptions about who students are and what they're thinking or feeling.
- ◆ create course assignments, assessments, and exams that support learning while further clarifying the content and dialogue covered in the course.
- ◆ equip my students with tools to process their thoughts and opinions inside and outside of the classroom.
- ◆ encourage my students to think like they think, not think like I think (or how I think they're supposed to think).
- ◆ teach my students how to have honest, intellectually stimulating, interpersonal classroom conversations about race without minimizing reality, or dismissing unfamiliar perspectives and experiences.
- ◆ incorporate current events without pushing a personal agenda (again).
- ◆ carve out enough space for the feelings each student brings to the conversation while keeping learning at the fore.
- ◆ deal with me, and the very real truth that in order to give any of this to my students, I needed to be willing to give these things to myself.

Have mercy on us all. I genuinely didn't know if I could pull this off. The prospect of taking this on was terrifying. Overwhelming. Intimidating.

Just like it might feel intimidating for you to pick up this book. Like you're making some sort of commitment to transform yourself into a Superhero Brave Educator who always knows exactly what to do when a sticky conversation about race comes up in the classroom. (Insert cheesy superhero pose with theme song here.) Welp, here's some good news. I made mistakes—lots of mistakes. I didn't get everything right. There was so much

I didn't know, and so much I still don't know. But I did begin to find my way through. I remember how lonely and weary I felt along the way. I felt so lost. So, so lost. That's why I'm writing these words to you. That's why we're having this conversation in this way. Because I know what it's like to discover that all your education, your experience, your exposure, and your eloquence haven't prepared you for the mechanics of navigating this conversation. You are not alone. You're not the only educator who feels overwhelmed by the prospect of leading and navigating classroom conversations about race. You deserve honest companionship along the way. So with your permission I'd like to tell you more about the path I stumbled down.

Something extraordinary happened, completely unplanned. Birthed directly from my willingness to grapple with not having all the answers *for the first time in my life*, I began to create practical tools and techniques for talking about race in the classroom that generated connection, learning, belonging, and discovery instead of shame and separation. Because I dove in headfirst and got so incredibly lost along the way, I had no choice but to pay really close attention to what was happening in my classroom. Looking reality straight in the face helped me begin to *directly experience* what worked and what didn't work for my students. I listened, lead class each day, administered assignments and exams, and inhaled their verbal and nonverbal feedback. Paying such close attention helped me build connection. Connecting with my students taught me *what* I needed to do and *how* I needed to do it. I could *see* in live time which choices opened classroom dialogue and what shut my students down. I was learning how to navigate race conversations in the classroom *by doing it*, not by climbing up on my I Know Everything Pedestal and pretending to have all the answers. Inviting my students to be equal participants in the journey of learning how to have this conversation transformed the entire process, and taught me how to equip myself and my students with the tools we needed to create productive dialogue instead of combatation.

Making listening a priority and focusing my energy on shaping the tools I needed to be an effective facilitator of their learning resulted in a dynamic, interactive classroom that had space for students to speak, think, ask hard questions, learn, discover, share, and weave stories together—regardless of where students fell along social, racial, ethnic, religious, political, sexual, gender, economic, age, or additional/overlapping spectra. Discovering that I didn't know where to begin, and embracing the journey of finding my way through, led to yet another unexpected (but challenging) upside; I was so internally raw and vulnerable that I became aware of *how important it was for me to avoid constantly filling our shared classroom space with my insecurities and fears.* The more I learned to separate my fear of failure from my teaching, the deeper we dove into engaging classroom conversations.

This entire experience felt completely outside-the-box. None of this fell under the definition of what I was "supposed to be doing" as an educator. The whole thing was a risk. I didn't know what the results would be. To my extreme shock, over the course of three semesters (and creating two separate courses at the intersection of race and the law from scratch) students said things like:

> Professor Cobran is literally the best professor I have had so far. She knows the material intimately and steers the students to better understand it themselves as well. She always makes sure that we understand the material as we're talking about it in class and is always available to assist us however she professionally can.

> The course was overall challenging. A lot of confusing material and difficult to understand, especially for my first case law class. However, due to Professor Cobran's teaching style and use of challenging everyone's critical thinking skills, but also keeping us focused on what was important, allowed me to learn a great deal and overall enjoying this class.

> Professor Cobran was an excellent professor. The course material can be extremely demanding and difficult to understand but she really helped me to understand. She really taught me how to think critically.

The case law in this class was very difficult, but professor did a great job at breaking it down. I have learned a lot about the material.

Professor Cobran was AWESOME and I really enjoyed taking this class. She tailored the material to what she felt was more important to cover and what we, the students, wanted to learn more in-depth. She was really helpful and always available in terms of assisting us with papers, debates, etc.

I loved this course along with the set up and how flexible it was. I enjoyed being able to change things based on our discussions.

Professor Cobran is one of the best professors I have ever had. She facilitates constructive and challenging discussions and is an exceptional instructor.

Easily the most important class I've ever taken. Helped develop critical thinking skills and arguing valid points.

Professor Cobran is one of the best professors that I have ever been able to learn from. She is extremely intelligent and is very caring of all her students.

I have taken Professor Cobran two semesters in a row now and she is to date my favorite professor I've had the pleasure of studying under. She is always incredibly professional, but also incredibly helpful and genuine in her concern for her students' understanding of the material and their wellbeing.

I genuinely thought there wasn't structure to the course at first, but there really is. Much more critical thinking and discussion rather than just straight power point and facts. It made the class challenging but very engaging and AWESOME!

Professor Cobran is hands down one of the best professors I've ever had. She genuinely cared about us but
didn't go easy on us. You could tell she wanted us to
think and learn for ourselves. I felt that the tests were fair
and I really appreciate that she blind-graded our assignments. I am so grateful for the skills this class has taught
me!

She was a great professor! Incredibly intelligent and
thought-provoking. I liked the format of the class but only
wish we did more in smaller groups to allow more discussion. Really enjoyed and will recommend the course.

Professor Cobran did an excellent job of using in-class
questions and discussion rather than lecture. The course
felt like an exploration and discovery rather than listening and learning.

Professor Cobran is one of the most engaging professors
I have encountered in my college experience. She actively
encourages a comfortable environment for diverse conversation while going in-depth to very important subject
matter.

I sat in my car shaking my head with tears in my eyes. I read
and re-read these evaluations to verify they existed on paper and
not in my imagination. Apparently, I was very, very wrong about
needing to have all the answers. As it turns out, my not knowing
where to start was exactly the start we needed to create learning,
connection, and shared experiences in our conversations about
race in the classroom.

Our Failures Are Trying to Give Us Gifts

People often ask how I ended up in this line of work. This strikes
me as a valid question, since under no circumstances was any of
this part of my grand plan. My short answer is that learning how

to talk about race with students in classrooms saved me from who I was pretending to become. Releasing the pressure of trying to be who I thought I was supposed to be helped me discover that it was possible for people from many different backgrounds and perspectives to have conversations about race where we feel mutually seen, heard, respected, supported, and understood. As a writer, teacher, consultant, and speaker, I create conversations about race where we can connect more and fear less. Conversations where we learn together, and grow as we truly see each other. There are no words to describe the joy my soul feels when we recognize our capability to have conversations about race that create connection *whether or not we agree.*

All of my failure, every moment I believed I was wrong because I didn't know, every ounce of pressure I placed on myself to perform because I thought I *had* to have all the answers became valuable experience I use throughout my work and teaching. My experience of failure helped me identify exactly how I didn't want my students to feel in my classroom. Letting go of my belief that not knowing equals failure helped me design a classroom environment filled with conversations about race where students discovered that *not knowing is an invitation to learn.*

Crucial Tip
Not knowing is where discovery begins.

I am eternally grateful to my students because their feedback is a gigantic piece of why you and I are having this conversation in the way we're having it. Conversations with educators helped me understand that I wasn't the only one feeling lonely and unsupported as I tried to figure all this out. So I write to you as a human who has sat right where you are, who is intimately familiar with the determination required to find a way forward in the face of uncertainty. I know what it's like to feel judged instead of supported, ignored instead of listened to. I know the feeling of being incredibly lost, yet still responsible for leading and teaching and creating classroom experiences where students can grow, and hopefully, thrive. I'm not writing this book from a pedestal. I'm writing this book sitting right here, next to you.

Here's How This Book Exists to Support You

The Brave Educator is not another line on your to-do list. It's not filled with statistical analyses. There are no literature reviews. I haven't done a point-by-point breakdown of alternative approaches, then conducted multiple regression or cost–benefit analyses examining the pros and cons of each. I respect and deeply value each of these techniques and methods of analysis. They are valid, essential, and important. We need them.

That's just not what this book is about.

We're going to have this conversation from a different starting point. We're going to begin at an alternate beginning. We're going to begin by admitting that we just don't know. Then we're going to keep breathing and walking through our journey of discovery. Through vulnerable conversation together, we'll carve a path through that makes sense for you and your students in your classroom. This book is adaptable. It's personal. It's constructed around stories, conversations, mistakes, examples, scripts, tools for connection, and lessons learned through my face-first stumble into strategies for conversations about race that work in real classrooms with real students.

I'm not interested in shaming you for what you don't know. (My shame certainly didn't help me be more productive.) I'm not interested in promoting my approach as the best and only way. I don't believe that. I'm here to walk beside you and supply you with tools and support so that you can begin finding your way through. Take what works. Leave the rest. Treat this book like a good recipe, one that you can take and adapt based on the specific needs in your classroom. I'll give you a few core ingredients I've found to be indispensable, provide options and examples for how to use each ingredient, lay out some common pitfalls to avoid, do my best to make sure you feel heard, and give you guidelines to help you feel supported you as you practice talking about race in your classroom(s).

How to Use This Book

I'm here to listen to you. I've designed *The Brave Educator* to be interactive. (It's exhausting to be talked at.) So I've done my best to make this book feel like we're talking with each other.

Here are a few of the features you'll find throughout the book:

 Crucial Tips
> Key shifts you can make to avoid stumbles and reduce frustration

 Your Turn
> Practical exercises to help you take action as you build forward momentum

 Make Tiny Tweaks
> Doable, energizing shifts that can lead to massive change

 Share Your Story
> Invitations to continue the conversation, go deeper, and share your feelings and thoughts directly with me as you read this book

> Get Your Brave Educator Action Pack
> We all need a little extra support sometimes. Practical tools that help us create change with more ease and less stress. That's what the **Brave Educator Action Pack** is for. Download it for free at krystlecobran.com/the-brave-educator to get a bit of extra support as you read. It includes additional space for you to explore your responses and thoughts, plus a surprise bonus (or two).

Reach for *The Brave Educator* when you're in deep and you can't find up. Grab it when you're standing in the classroom and it feels like things are going sideways, quickly. Flip through it when you're creating your lesson plan, and you're just not sure how to navigate that sticky patch.

You're working hard to create a classroom environment that supports your students. *The Brave Educator* exists to support you.

This Is a Place for You to Begin

Nothing in this book rests on the presumption that I hold any magical answers, am the ultimate authority about anything, or am entitled to shame or judge you because of my expertise. I've attempted to create a book that helps you feel less blindsided by the realities of navigating race conversations in the classroom and done my best to avoid lecturing at you (hence the shameless violation of rules of grammar). When you pick up this book and read these pages, I want these words to release stress and relieve pressure, not induce more of it.

Use this book to explore and feel and discover and create conversations about race in the classroom in your own voice, using your own words, without fear. Use this book to start unpacking what you wish you knew so you can start dealing with what actually *is*. Get support, become equipped, and get empowered. Come back often.

You know all that work you put into creating a classroom environment where your students feel cared for and supported, all that energy and time you dedicate to keeping the classroom stable and safe? That's what *The Brave Educator* is for you. A space where *you* can learn. A spot where you can ask questions without being afraid, where you don't have to worry about what I'm thinking about you, or wonder whether your questions are dense and you should have already known the answer. (For the record, I do not feel this way about any of your questions. It's the antithesis of my work and who I am.)

Crucial Tip
This is a beginning, not an ending.

This is a place for you to begin. It's companionship and clarity. Usable tools. Doable tips. Grounded perspective with real-world examples designed to help you learn how to navigate conversations about race in the classroom.

So if you're looking for a comprehensive history of the intersection between racist ideas and educational outcomes or an in-depth examination of the historical, political, religious, cultural, and socioeconomic roots of racism and how pathways that perpetuate horrifically disparate outcomes been maliciously embedded into systems throughout American (and global) society while perpetuating various levels of wokeness and burden among racial and ethnic groups—I strongly recommend you put this book down immediately. I would be honored to have these conversations with you, but that's not the focus of this book. You will be sorely disappointed. I respect your time. Waiting for me to shame people (any human, including yourself) in these pages or expecting me to prescribe ways you can start fixing the people around you will mean waiting an unending wait. I'm going to let you down. *The Brave Educator* won't help you do any of things.

This book exists to help you learn how to begin finding your way through classroom conversations about race. That's it.

My hope is that this book feels strange to you—strangely refreshing, like opening windows and letting the crisp cold air of morning move through. Let's take turns listening and sharing so that I can see you, you can see me, and together we can connect and deliver the support you need.

 Make Tiny Tweaks

Less Strain, More Connection

Feeling like someone's chasing you down with a chainsaw screaming, *You're gonna mess this up!!!!!!* when race comes up in your classroom makes it difficult to learn, engage, discover, or create. Leading conversations about race under siege is like threading a needle on a roller coaster. The excessive tension makes us jumpy and prone to rapid evasive action. This setup doesn't lend itself well to being present either, which is essential in facilitating conversations about race in the classroom that generate connection.

So here's a tool you can use right now to make sure you don't poke yourself in the eye: **Practice being kind to yourself**. Yep. You read that correctly. Be kind. Breathe.

There are a few upsides (or more) to practicing kindness. You'll start to notice that the whole world feels a bit less irritating. You'll be more present. You'll have more fuel in your tank so that you can actually *listen*. And you'll probably have a little more energy to endure navigating challenging conversations about race with unpredictable human beings.

Section I

Two Tips to Give You a Solid Start

Solid Start Tip 1

Let's Try Listening to Each Other

Listen First

It was the fuzzy kind of rain, a wet that hugs your face and clings to your clothing. The sky, the color gray that makes beds look like heaven. When opening your car door feels like climbing into a wet mouth it's helpful to have someone you want to see on the other end. I was heading to meet my friend Alice (not her real name). She's been an educator for over a decade and was in the middle of surviving a particularly stressful day. Health challenges without clear resolutions. Life doesn't stop when we commit to the invisible labor of education. Making it through the chilly air wasn't much of a burden that day. Alice is open-hearted and generous, prone to wonder. She has the kind of joy for life that can startle us awake. Our conversations tend to flow free, wide, and deep; facing the unknown makes pain palpable, fears more shareable. We drifted, sharing laughter, tears, and frustrations.

Then there were words that broke through my listening. (My body is bracing.) Words describing what Alice is responsible for every single day as an educator. Preparing and writing curricula, responding to mountains of emails and requests, required training and seminars, surviving teacher evaluations, attempting to build nurturing parent–teacher relationships, coping with unpredictable (and sometimes unforeseeable) behavioral challenges, spending her own cash to make copies (because she's hit her allotment for the month but still needs to print worksheets for students) or because she sees that a student needs a coat to keep the cold wet out, navigating broken communication pipelines, needing help and not knowing who she can ask without risking being shamed, completing continuing education, adapting lessons and assignments to fit individual student needs, staying up late to create assignments based on requests (and then not receiving any feedback), dealing with constantly shifting standards right in the middle of attempting to create bonds of dependability and stability with students, feeling perpetually exhausted, needing practical training on how to implement all of the tools she's constantly being trained to use, running low on time, struggling to maintain perspective, craving assistance while feeling pressure to know all of the answers, all of the time. And we haven't even gotten to the actual teaching yet. Something about this conversation was eerily familiar. But something else about the *way* we were having this conversation shook my consciousness awake.

Training and Experience Aren't the Same Things

Law school gave me tools to think, research, study, logically analyze, and understand the law. But the actual mechanics, the real day-to-day grind and tiny details that add up to form the reality of practicing law were skills I couldn't even conceive I needed until I found myself knee-deep in beginning to understand just how much I didn't yet know as a judicial law clerk. Coming into this awareness was blindsiding and surprising. It's the journey between knowing and *knowing*. As we move away from thinking that being in possession of information is enough, we begin to grasp that information, when combined with our bumbling mistakes, delivers the perspective that only experience can bring. It's *inside* the process of taking action where we shift from being informed to becoming equipped. We mold our perspective as we move away from the sidelines (assuming we know what an experience is like) into being present (feeling our way through reality). Our expectations unravel as we navigate sticking points that feel uncontainable and unpredictable. This unraveling is what helps us connect with each other and stay engaged throughout the journey. Alice's words on this cold and wet day took me *inside* her experience. Turned her struggles as an educator from abstract and fleeting into pain that was touchable and real. As I looked at my friend run into these challenges face-first, I knew that courage was in front of me. A human choosing to get up every day and find a way where there is no way. Her words were so compelling that I wanted to act, to present an immediate solution in the moment, but what I needed to do was listen.

Reach for Listening Instead of Assumption

Crucial Tip
Listening is where everything begins.

The journey of going from knowing to *knowing* isn't one we need to go alone. When we listen to each other and share our experiences, we feel less isolated. Yet we resist listening. I certainly did. There are countless moments when I dismissed listening as secondary to productivity. *After all, isn't my job as an educator to teach the material, and forget about challenging feelings or difficulties I'm experiencing? I have to get through this. Who has time to listen anyway?* Maintaining a façade of strength can be seductive. But when we draw a false dividing line between the work of educating and the listening that helps us *be present* in our educational experiences, we sacrifice opportunities to close the gap between having information and understanding how to effectively use that information. Listening is at the core of true productivity in the classroom. Without listening, we keep *doing* without understanding what's happening either with us or with our students. Taking action without clarity about whether all our doing is creating the results we want to experience is an exercise in inefficiency and misdirected energy. Listening doesn't sound like a glamorous action step, but it's missing. It's missing from our strategic planning sessions. It's missing from our interpersonal conversations and the limited time allocated for classroom prep. When we skip listening, we miss out on climbing inside the reality of what's happening in our classrooms. That's when we start making recommendations and suggesting solutions without ever having uncovered what the real problems might be. We start turning ourselves and our students into equations we must somehow solve in five minutes or less. Then, in our frustration, we turn on each other because we feel completely and utterly alone.

When I reach for assumption before I listen to you, I miss deeply understanding the very real experiences you live while navigating conversations about race in the classroom. Part of why we avoid listening is because when we listen, we feel. We feel the frustration of knowing that we don't have the first idea about where to begin. We feel the overwhelming weight of needing to listen to our students so we can equip them not just to understand the course material but to communicate their thoughts and feelings effectively. And we feel all this in the middle of a conversation that most of us are incredibly uncomfortable with. I mean, let's face it. Of course this is hard. The race conversation isn't exactly a glowing example of how we've managed to come together across The Cultural Divide to listen, communicate, and empathize. We struggle with having real conversations about race as a culture; conversations that don't boil down to one person or group taking sides against another person or group. Whatever pressure we're feeling as a culture gets amplified within the classroom. Stakes are high. Demands are high. Eyeballs watching and ears listening for any sign of a misstep are plentiful. This means that on top of learning how to listen to our students so we can discover how to best meet their needs in the classroom, *we have to make it a priority to carve out space to listen to each other, and pay attention to our own needs if we're going to be able to endure this journey.*

Share Your Story

I want to listen to you. Go to krystlecobran.com/the-brave-educator to share your thoughts, your questions, your concerns, and your stories with me.

Feelings Are Important

I am intimately familiar with the impulse to pretend feelings don't matter. *Feelings are fluffy things that only people with the luxury of extra time spend time thinking about.* Feeling isn't my favorite go-to when I'm presented with a challenge. Avoiding feeling and conjuring up a brilliant solution seems way more enjoyable. But when I avoid *feeling* and stay hyper-focused on *doing,* I avoid listening, which means I avoid discovering the lessons I need to learn; lessons that transform impossible conversations about race into opportunities to create dialogue that reduces combat and promotes learning.

On top of the reality that we tend to treat being an educator as synonymous with being super-productive robots devoid of basic human needs and feelings, most of what educators do is invisible: the training, the prep, the million-and-one adjustments in a day, the balancing countless needs and demands simultaneously. Education is work that demands quiet efficiency. In the middle of all this sits the looming fear that something might go wrong at any moment. In this context, the Pressure of Perfection is a curling finger, pulling us toward pretending that everything is OK, we've got it all under control, pointing us away from learning how to navigate the complex challenges before us.

Educators aren't exempt from human feeling and emotion. *Educators are humans with needs who teach other humans with needs.*

Not Listening Costs Us More Than We Think

There are few things worse than trying to learn from someone who refuses to listen. The gap between listening and scanning to verify our assumptions frays our ability to connect. Vital information we need to create learning and discovery in the classroom falls by the wayside.

The power of listening is jarring. Not listening disrupts everything: connection, introspection, openness to creating new solutions and learning new skills, cultivation of independent thinking, discovering the nuances around how to navigate conversations about race in your specific classroom, understanding how to connect dialogue to course content, asking important clarifying questions . . . everything. The moment we stop listening is the moment we start talking *at* our students and past each other. It's a draining experience. And that's how we've been telling ourselves we're supposed to navigate conversations about race. We've been pretending that the classroom is some sort of bizarre alternate reality where educators aren't humans with lives and feelings, students should magically manufacture skills for productive conversations about race while we talk at them (and when we haven't yet agreed about how to talk about race as a culture), and educators must divine a complete understanding about how to make those conversations happen out of thin air while successfully managing all of their preexisting responsibilities and simultaneously cultivating the skills necessary to make productive conversations happen. This is a setup for looping frustration and circular conversations that head nowhere, fast.

 Your Turn

Permission to Feel

*Grab something to write with and your **Brave Educator Action Pack** (get your free download at krystlecobran.com/the-brave-educator).*

Take 10 minutes to complete the following exercise.

1. Take a deep breath.
2. Take a moment to think about your classroom environment, yourself, your teaching, and your students.

3. Now, how would you feel if you were a student in your classroom having a conversation about race?

4. Answer the following prompt: In my classroom, students feel _____ [insert feelings you've observed, or that students have shared with you].

Take a moment to notice how you're feeling. Be gentle with yourself. Take another deep breath.

5. Answer this prompt: I want my students to feel _____ [insert ways you want students to feel in your classroom].

6. Warning: This question will tick you off. You will not want to answer it.

How do you need to take care of yourself and your feelings so you can show up in class ready to meet students where they are?

Write down everything that comes to mind. Be specific.

7. Look at the list you created. Pick one thing. Go do something kind for yourself.

So we're going to try something different. We're going to reach for listening. We're going to listen when we're feeling uncomfortable, we're going to listen when our students ask a question we don't know the answer to, we're going to listen when we feel completely unprepared to lead, we're going to listen when a student says something that catches us by surprise, we're going to listen when that internal ding goes off telling us we're in serious need of clarity and practical support, and we're going to listen when everything around us says to push our perspective, our agenda, our thoughts into the minds of our students and instead use the power of listening to make a conscious choice to prioritize student learning. We're going to begin with listening so we don't remain trapped in assumption-fueled judgment. And we're going to start practicing right now, with you listening to you.

 Make Tiny Tweaks

Start Listening to Yourself

Listening to yourself is essential. In recent years, I began to notice how much I believed that working hard was the same thing as never stopping, never sitting still and listening to what I was feeling or thinking. (You should have seen me freaking out as I wrote this book.) I felt this need to *Be productive!!* and kept loading pressure on myself to produce. But the truth is that my productivity was enhanced, not limited, when I took time to think, feel, and be *in* the process. Walking outside, looking up at the sky, staring at tree leaves through a window, taking a moment to laugh, sipping a good cup of tea, and writing down a quick thought in a notebook are all things I've found help me stop ignoring my own voice so that I can start learning from my experiences. You can do this. You can take a minute out of your day to listen to a podcast you love on your commute, take a quick walk during lunch, or keep a small notebook on hand where you can write down snippets that come to you throughout the day. It's not luxurious. It's practicing the very behaviors—thinking, processing, and taking responsibility for our own feelings—we want our students to practice.

Solid Start Tip 2

Let's Make Room for Discovery

Give Judgment a Break

Judgment turns dialogue into debate, conversation into combat. If you read this book focusing on all the things you think you need to prove you already know, or on all the things that you wish you knew that you don't know, or on all the things you think you need to fix about yourself (or anyone else for that matter), you'll feel like a ping-pong ball with judgment on one side of the table and defensiveness on the other. To avoid this scenario, we're going to turn judgment into discovery. Yes. You read that correctly. We're basically transforming judgment into a vehicle for discovery. Not because everything is all right and we just need to hum and sing songs to make the world a better place (that's a hard no), but because in this conversation, *judgment that stops us from connecting and engaging is a barrier, not a stepping-stone to real conversation.* The ways we judge ourselves become powerful filters that stop us from discovering what's right in front of us, blocking us from experiencing the reality that surrounds us. Our internal judgment generates outward defensiveness.

Our outward defensiveness shuts down classroom conversation. Judgment and defensiveness are not good conversation partners. These two are a combo that can knock conversation and connection off the rails before we've even had a chance to get the classroom dialogue started.

 ## Your Turn

10 Things You're Going to Stop Judging Yourself For

*Grab something to write with and your **Brave Educator Action Pack** (get your free download at krystlecobran.com/the-brave-educator).*

I can feel your resistance. To help you through this process, I've created a handy list of 10 things you're not going to judge yourself for as you read this book.

Fill in the blank with the items that resonate with you.

I am not going to judge myself for _____
_____ [fill in the blank using the list below].

1. What I wish I knew about race that I don't yet know.
2. What I need to know about race that I don't yet understand.
3. What I want to understand about race that I don't know how to discover.
4. What I wish I'd done in that conversation that I didn't.
5. What I wish I'd said in that conversation that I didn't say.
6. Recognizing I've been silent and need to learn how to speak up.
7. When I felt completely out of my depth and was embarrassed because of it.
8. When I didn't know how to respond to that parent or student in that conversation.
9. When I realized that my lived experiences are not the same as my students' lived experiences.
10. That moment I realized I had no idea where to begin.

While you're releasing judgment, I need to tell you that I have no interest in judging you. We're officially declaring this a judgment-free zone. This might feel ridiculous, but it's important. When we're busy judging ourselves, we're probably judging our students, which means we're not actually listening. When we're not really listening, we're doing what we think we're supposed to be doing instead of responding to student needs. When we're not responding to students' needs, we're not connecting. And when we're not connecting it's nearly impossible to learn how to lead honest conversations about race in the classroom. Being fixated on judgment messes with our ability to listen to stay present and responsive. What we bring into our classroom has the power to shape our entire classroom environment. A classroom filled with lively and engaging dialogue, where students actively and willingly participate, doesn't happen because we've mastered the art of judgment.

Crucial Tip
When we're judging, we're not connecting.

Judgment is the red carpet that paves the way for disconnection to come dancing down the aisle. The problem isn't that we aren't capable of having the conversation. The problem isn't that students aren't capable of having the conversation. The problem isn't that we're so divided as a culture that real conversation about race is impossible. Being so deeply preoccupied with judging each other and ourselves that we end up depriving ourselves of the tools, support, and opportunities we need to learn how to navigate conversations about race in the classroom *is a problem*. Judgment that functions as a barrier to connection doesn't facilitate our growth as educators or promote student learning. This is the kind of judgment that makes us want to avoid the race conversation in its entirety.

When we cling to judgment because we feel fear and we aren't sure where to start, we get stuck in overwhelm and distraction instead of effectively moving through the process of learning how to lead conversations about race in the classroom.

We sink into silence. Pile more pressure on ourselves to perform. Dodge the conversation. Tiptoe around the edges. Swallow the shame of not knowing how to do something that we were all supposed to know how to do *without ever having had the opportunity to learn how to do it*. It. Is. So. Frustrating. Learning how to move through classroom conversations about race is a learned skill. I repeat. It's a *learned skill*. I know this because I've lived it. I stood in front of a classroom, responsible for building and teaching a course called Race & the Law—from scratch. (There's a more extensive version of this story in the Introduction.) It was terrifying. I dove face-first into it. (We can discuss my sanity at another point in time.) Creating conversations about race that are productive, educational, and empowering, while we proactively facilitate student learning, begins when we release the expectation that we're already supposed to know how to make it happen and instead *give ourselves permission to learn how to do it by doing it*. The judgment that silences, makes us want to curl into a ball, disengage, and stops us from taking another step down the path. It leads us away from deeper connection with our students, ourselves, and our skill sets. This letting go of judgment thing sounds strange. But it works. Put it in the category of Weird But Worth It. Releasing judgment creates freedom for educators to engage, and helps us let go of a barrier that keeps us trapped in the cycle of avoiding the very skills we so desperately want to learn. Learning by doing (within the context of healthy responsibility and boundaries) can be powerful. When instead of *doing* we spend our energy judging ourselves, we miss out on discovery—one of the best parts of the journey.

Crucial Tip
What we pretend to already know becomes what we cannot learn.

Releasing judgment also helps us create classroom conversations that are more about learning and connection than defending our insecurities. You're probably feeling pretty skeptical right at this moment, but I'm asking you to give turning judgment into discovery a try anyway. Start with the next five minutes. Then try another five minutes. Then another. Practice transforming judgment into discovery as you read each page of this book. I've created this easy-to-do exercise to help you get rolling.

 Your Turn

Let's Turn Judgment Into Discovery
*Grab something to write with and your **Brave Educator Action Pack** (get your free download at krystlecobran.com/the-brave-educator).*

◆ Pull out a piece of paper and a pen.
◆ Write the word JUDGMENT at the very top. (Preferably in big capital letters.)
◆ Answer this question: When it comes to classroom conversations about race, I'm failing because I don't know _____
_____.
◆ Write down everything that comes to mind. Everything you judge yourself for when race comes up.
◆ Keep writing.
◆ Take a deep breath.
◆ Anything else come to mind?

Now take a look at the list you've created—a good hard look.

◆ Take your pen, and cross out JUDGMENT at the top.
◆ Write DISCOVERY next to the (now-)crossed-out ~~JUDGMENT.~~
◆ Cross out the "When it comes to classroom conversations race" question prompt. Make sure you cross out the whole thing.
◆ Write this prompt next to the old prompt: I get to discover _____ about leading classroom conversations about race.
◆ Now, out loud (don't do this while operating anything that moves please), put what you wrote into the "_____" of the new prompt.

For example, if you wrote,

> When it comes to classroom conversations about race, I'm failing because I don't know how to deal with race when it comes up in unexpected ways.

replace it with:

> I get to discover how to deal with classroom conversations about race when it comes up in unexpected ways.

Do this for every item on your list.

The goal: Reframe what you don't know as an invitation to move toward discovery and away from judgment.

Use this exercise every time you find yourself reaching for judgment instead of discovery when race comes up in the classroom.

Is It Really Fair for Us to Stop Judging Ourselves?

I can hear your brain. I hear you wondering whether my asking you to give judgment a break is really fair in light of the immeasurable and ongoing suffering people from communities of color have lived with for centuries. I understand, and your desire to dive to deeper depths of healthy, non-debilitating empathy is one I respect and encourage.

But how does the judgment that stops us from engaging in conversations about race get us any closer to understanding human stories we're unfamiliar with? Stories our students are living, stories that we see on the news and struggle to comprehend? Stories we live daily? Stories we so desperately want to understand but haven't yet found a way to connect with?

How does judgment that distances us from connecting with ourselves and our students improve one ounce of our teaching, decision-making, or leadership?

When we practice shutting ourselves down with judgment, it doesn't take long before we're doling out to everyone else what we're giving to ourselves. It's like training for a marathon. If we get up every day and run a thousand Let Me Judge Me miles, it's going to be really hard to turn to our students (or colleagues) in a moment of difficult conversation about race and start with listening and connecting instead of dismissing and judging. After all, isn't judgment what we've trained ourselves to do?

There will be ups, and there will be downs in this process. But if we approach the highs and lows and everything in between with an attitude of discovery (instead of judgment), we'll begin to notice that we're *actually having real conversations about race instead of thinking about how much we need to have them.*

 Your Turn

Make a Shift When Judgment Is Stressing You Out

*Grab something to write with and your **Brave Educator Action Pack** (get your free download at krystlecobran.com/the-brave-educator).*

Turning discomfort into discovery means coming face-to-face with how uncomfortable the race conversation in the classroom can be. Since judging ourselves or our students isn't as productive as we'd like it to be, we need to find a way to reduce stress and shift our perspective when things get overwhelming. I created this exercise to help. Perspective is not a joke. If you're unkind to yourself as you learn how to navigate race in the classroom you're not going to be motivated for the journey. And I assure you, learning how to navigate race in the classroom is a journey.

Use this exercise to hit reset whenever you're feeling stressed:
    OK, _____[your name goes here], I'm feeling pretty stressed about this conversation. I really wish I didn't have to talk about this. I wish the reality of our world and

culture were different. I wish I could pretend this conversation wasn't necessary, but that would be a denial of real human experiences, including my own. Since that's not something I'm interested in, I need to find another way through this.

I'm uncomfortable about _____ [insert what makes you uncomfortable here]. I get it. I've got no judgment for you. How you feel is how you feel. The good news, _____ [insert your name here]? I get to make a choice about what happens next.

I choose to be kind to me by _____ [insert way you're going to be kind to yourself here]. I'm going to learn more about _____ [insert thing you're afraid of in the race conversation here] by _____ [insert things you're going to do to learn more here]. I understand that navigating conversations about race is a journey—something I'm currently learning how to do and will continue to learn for the rest of my life.

I'm taking tangible action by _____ [insert choice you're making instead of judging yourself here]. Plus, there's more good news. Everything I discover is an experience, a lesson, a tool, information, vital perspective that I can use to support my growth and serve my students in the classroom.

Let's practice transforming judgment into discovery so that we can create room to listen, talk, and connect, with ourselves, our students, and each other.

Feel that breath of fresh air? That waft of possibility? Take a deep breath.

That's what we're going for.

And if you're really worried about letting judgment go because you're craving a heaping helping, I'm certain you can find some on the Internet somewhere. I don't recommend it, though.

Make Tiny Tweaks

Take a Moment to Care for You

Something about being an educator positions us to get real finicky about taking care of ourselves. The grind and responsibilities of education never stop. In this realm of ever-escalating demands, it's easy to conflate commitment to positive student outcomes with never stopping. Never pausing to refuel. This is a recipe for exhaustion, depletion, rage, and volcanic frustration. So I'm going to ask you to do something. Go do something pleasant, an activity that has nothing to do with the daily obligations you face every day, that makes your heart glow and your mind go still for a second. I personally enjoy sitting in dark movie theaters. Getting outside to be in the green or look up (or down) at the blue can be a surprising reset. A good cup of tea can do wonders. (I would make you a fresh pot of lemon ginger tea if I could.) Whatever you choose, *do* something that's nourishing, healthy, and safe for you. And don't spend one iota of a second judging yourself for it.

Section II

Your Flexible Four-Step Road Map

Step 1

Three Words to Help Keep Student Learning at the Center

When the Pressure We're Putting on Ourselves Affects Our Classrooms

My students were entirely too quiet. I stood at the front of the room, material for the day up on the projector, looking at a room full of humans working really hard at avoiding eye contact. It was still early in the semester, but we'd already begun establishing rapport. Opening the course with conversations about TED Talks helped loosen things up, establish that I was more interested in productive dialogue than in proving that my thoughts were the ones my students should think. So on this particular day, I was perplexed. *Why are they so quiet?* I couldn't figure it out. As my confusion grew, I decided to just, well, ask. Somewhere in the awkward exchange that followed, I caught a glimpse of someone—Me. I saw my fear. My fear of being wrong, of making a mistake. And it dawned on me that I was overcompensating. I was so concerned with looking like I had it all together that I was projecting an image. An over-inflated mirage of being filled with endless answers and no unresolved questions. My insecurity-fueled pretense was eating the possibility of connection alive.

The image I was projecting turned up the pressure in the room. Without meaning to, *I was actively discouraging openness and curiosity because I was consumed with how I looked in the conversation.*

Witnessing the impact of my fear caught me by surprise. But is it really? When I think back to the educators who positively influenced me as a student, it's the humans who showed up with honesty and wise transparency who left the biggest impact. These educators weren't busy projecting an image. Their energy was focused on other priorities. On stimulating our (the students') minds, empowering our capability, equipping us with analytical skills, and challenging us to take charge of our own learning. These brilliant and flawed human beings walked into classrooms, offered us their imperfect selves, and changed our lives forever. (I'm still learning lessons from them, even now.) There's something sacred about seeing the humanity in a teacher that unlocks vulnerability in the classroom. Honest teachers with healthy boundaries shift the dynamic of learning within the four walls, transforming the process of uncovering new knowledge from cold and detached to engaging and mind-opening.

The truth is that my fear took root long before I walked into class that day. I was fueling it with my approach toward preparing for class.

I was beyond nervous. On top of walking students through nuanced conversations about race, core reading material for the course came from Supreme Court cases. Which meant that I was responsible for equipping undergraduate students with the skills needed to read and analyze case law, and I had to figure out how to teach the importance of context (social, political, historical, cultural, economic, etc.), framing, and precedent. I also needed to create an open, dialogue-driven classroom environment, while finding a way to make layered and complex material accessible so that students felt engaged and empowered as we moved through the course. This task was daunting, and I'd never seen it done before. (I learned how to read case law in law school, not in undergrad.) Terrified of failing or letting my students down, I assumed I wasn't up to the challenge since I couldn't think of every answer to every single question a student might ask as I prepared for class. There was so much more prep I wanted to do before standing in front of the classroom. I felt inept and overwhelmed, and it wasn't pleasant. And I most definitely didn't want any of my students to pick up on my insecurities. So I reached into my old How-Can-I-Survive-Life-While-Concealing-All-My-Weaknesses Toolkit and pulled out one of my performance masks—more specifically, my Look-At-Me-I-Have-All-the-Answers-I'm-So-Fly-No-One-Can-Faze-Me Mask.

I wanted to feel less vulnerable. I wanted to feel safer: safe from judgment, safe from the risk of failure, safe from being seen in my struggle.

I'd bought into the myth that being strong means looking strong at all times. Projecting strength meant pretending to know even when I didn't. I don't know where or how it happened, but somewhere along the line, being a qualified educator merged with the utterly unrealistic expectation that I was required to exist as all-knowing sentient being in the classroom. This was too much pressure to keep contained. It spilled right out, into my classroom without me having to say a word about it.

The Importance of Giving Ourselves Permission to Not Have All the Answers

Before the day I caught my insecurities flying high, I'd asked Stefanie Lindquist (then Dean of the School of Public and International Affairs at the University of Georgia) for advice, and she gave me a priceless tip:

If a student asks you a question and you don't know the answer, say *I don't know. Let me do some research and get back to you.* Be honest when you don't know. Admit it.

The advice stuck. I could not shake it. There was something freeing about knowing that I could say the words *I don't know* without the world simultaneously coming to an apocalyptic end. The more I thought about it, the more I realized I needed to run toward the possibility of not knowing, because *not knowing is the key that opens the door to learning.* Being willing to admit when I didn't know created room for me to ask difficult questions and wrestle with the material; some of the precise behaviors I so badly wanted to nurture in my students.

As I worked on formatting my course, I knew I had to come up with a way to help my students and myself get more comfortable with the words *I don't know* ASAP. This could not be some hidden secret that students mysteriously stumbled upon. Somehow, I had to establish that in our classroom, *I didn't have all the answers and I didn't expect my students to either.* And I had to make it clear at the very beginning.

 Share Your Story

What scares you the most about leading conversations about race in the classroom? You're not the only one. Share your story with me at krystlecobran.com/the-brave-educator.

I decided to communicate it clearly. Directly. Out loud. On the first day of class. Standing in front of everyone. *I don't have all the answers, and I don't expect you to either.*

Establishing my classroom as a place where we all had permission to not know helped lead us toward honest conversations; all of which helped students think on their own much more than my standing in the front of classroom asking students to conform themselves to my (as-yet-undiscovered) divine opinions could.

To set students free to develop their own thoughts and practice effective communication in the classroom, we (educators) need to find a way to (a) help students experience being wrong as an opportunity to learn and then (b) eliminate students' fear of being shamed for their wrongness as early and quickly as we can.

What the Pressure of Having to Be Perfect All the Time Does to Our Teaching

There's that curling finger again; the Pressure of Perfection, pulling us toward pretending *Everything is all right; we've got it all under control. Nothing to see here.* We're supposed to know everything, and if we don't, fake it until we convince ourselves and everyone around us that we are the most brilliant thing since grass decided to be green. It doesn't work. This pressure pulls us away from connecting with our own stories and blocks us from accurately witnessing the stories of our students. It consumes us and eats away at our thinking, swallowing our words, all while depleting our energy. Trying to be perfect in the classroom is an exercise in isolation, at best; a lesson in deception, at worst. Combining this pressure with the preexisting pressure that comes with navigating conversations about race in the classroom is about as productive as having a root canal outdoors in a thunderstorm.

Under this ballooning pressure, classroom conversations about race become a game where we can't connect, create productive dialogue, or find our way through sticky conversations without resorting to pretending, shaming, or dismissing each other's perspectives. When we're consumed with being right, it's really hard to be attentive and responsive. The need to be right and have the answers makes us reactive, inclined to prioritize our position far more than our teaching.

There was nothing wrong with my students on the day they were excessively quiet. There was nothing wrong with me either. What I needed was to carve out space where I could process the fear I was feeling so that my fear didn't dictate how I showed up in the classroom. My attitude, my voice, my degree of eye contact, whether I was present and listening (versus distracted and disengaged), and my ability to connect and respond and listen to what my students were *actually* saying were setting the tone in the room. I needed to embrace the process of learning how to lead conversations about race in the classroom just as much as I was asking my students to embrace the process of learning the content we were covering. My resistance to saying *I don't know. Let me know some research and get back to you on that* was hampering my teaching.

I needed to take my own advice and remember what I said to my students at the beginning of the course.

I don't have all the answers, and I don't expect you to either.

Crucial Tip
It's difficult to give our students what
we refuse to give ourselves.

Start Releasing Pressure by Checking Your Expectations

I'd taken time to think about the environment I wanted to create
for my students. But I'd barely given any thought to how I needed
to support myself if I truly wanted to support my students.

If I was serious about what I said (about not having all the
answers), then I needed to make sure I wasn't just extending this
generosity to my students; I needed to give it to myself. I needed
to let go of expecting to have all of the answers all of the time.

Unrealistically expecting myself to know the answer to my
students' questions before they'd even asked fed the pressure to
pretend. This pressure wasn't helping my students learn, and it
wasn't helping me move toward the goals I'd set for my classroom. It was keeping me afraid, draining the life out of my classroom and the energy out of me.

Educators struggle to give to students what we refuse to give
to ourselves. Refusing to give ourselves permission to learn how
to honestly process, breathe, think, decide, create, listen, and
learn, as we discover how to create conversations about race in
the classroom makes it really hard for us to help our students
through unpredictable conversations about race.

Once we start compensating for our fear by pretending we've
got it all covered, the Pressure Rules take over. They're always
whispering in the background during classroom conversations
about race.

Your Turn

The Pressure Rules
Rule 1: Never act like you don't have the answers.
Rule 2: Just get along. But remember to prove a point.

Rule 3: Never complain in groups where people from different racial and ethnic backgrounds are present.

Rule 4: Buck up; be tough.

Rule 5: Find a solution; be strong. And if you don't find a solution and you need one, pretend you found one anyway.

Rule 6: Appearances first.

Rule 7: Just get it done. Perform. Even when hyperventilating and/losing every shred of your health and well-being, never, ever tell anyone how you're really feeling.

Rule 8: Wrap it up in a nice, neat bow.

Rule 9: The title of Educator means you're supposed to act like you've got it all figured out. Put on the show.

The Pressure Rules don't keep us safe. They don't facilitate learning. The more we give in to the pressure to put on a show, the less our students engage. *Pretending to have the answers becomes a veneer that blocks learning.* It builds a cloudy glass between us and our students, making it so that we can't hear them clearly.

Crucial Tip
Our leadership strengthens when we work together to discover what we don't know.

Teaching while overwhelmed by the Pressure Rules makes it difficult to create productive classroom conversations about race. (This is why it's profoundly important for educators to have spaces where we can have honest conversations about what the experience of learning how to create conversations about race in the classroom is really like. We need to know we're not alone.)

Your Turn

Ways We Can Respond to the Pressure (Two Simple Examples)

1. Shut down and reach for judgment.

Student says something about race that triggers you.
You (internally): *I wonder what this student is thinking. I should know what this student is thinking. I shouldn't ask my students about what they're thinking. Oh my gosh, I have to find a way to fix what this student is thinking. But I'm not even sure what I think about what the student just said. I can't do this. I'm failing.*

2. Reach for healthy curiosity and create a connection.

Student says something about race that triggers you.
You (internally): *I wonder what the student is thinking. Does this statement reduce human dignity or disrespect human experiences? No. I don't know what this student is thinking. I'll ask.*
You (ask student): What made you ask/say _____ [insert thing student asked/said] about _____ [insert race-related topic you're discussing in class]? (**<u>Listen</u>**. Engage with what is presented.) Then ask, Now that we've been talking about this a bit, let's explore how _____ [insert student's question/statement here] and _____ [reference related material you've already covered] connect.

Share Your Story

Have you ever sat through a moment of awkward silence in your classroom? Go to krystlecobran.com/the-brave-educator and share your thoughts and experiences with me.

When it's not working, don't pretend it is. I could've brushed past my students' silence that day, told myself it had nothing to do with me and everything to do with them, blamed it on the difficulties that come with navigating conversations about race and pointed my finger at our broader culture as the reason I was struggling in the classroom. I could have kept beating myself up for not having all the answers, walked out, and quit trying. But none of those choices respond to what my students were asking me for with their silence. My students were inviting me to try something new.

When Students Are Quiet, They're Trying to Tell Us Something

Student silence is information, not a verdict of failure. And it was information I desperately needed to make effective choices about how to structure and shape our classroom dialogue. The quiet was direct feedback telling me to try a different approach; to Make Tiny Tweaks. Shifting the dynamic of our classroom begins with me. My choices. I needed to teach students how to engage with the learning process by willingly engaging myself.

Practicing the curiosity we want our students to embrace gives them permission to treat the learning process as a Path of Discovery instead of a high-stress balancing act. We create a classroom where we can grow together as we learn together instead of focusing on trying to impress each other.

Crucial Tip
Education becomes just a bit more doable when we stop pretending we know everything.

Fear pushes us toward lecturing *at* (instead of connecting with) students. Sometimes, when we pummel ourselves for not having all the answers, we inadvertently begin pummeling students with our knowledge in an attempt to prove our capability. We try to lecture students into dialogue, into opening up, into sharing, and into engagement. But that's not typically how human beings work. (I certainly have no desire to open up and connect when I'm being intellectually pummeled.) Instead of beating ourselves up for not having all the answers, let's choose to extend the kindness to ourselves that we want to extend to our students. Let's reach for dialogue instead of a lecture (in an attempt to mask our fear).

Open conversation can change everything when we feel stuck in classroom conversations about race. My students didn't have a ton of words when I asked them why they were so quiet, but the words they did share gave me what I needed to keep tweaking my approach. Over the course of the semester, as I began asking my students more frequently and more openly to *tell me what they needed*, our conversations about race expanded. Became more lively. Downright fun, even. Instead of the classroom being a place where I was trapped under the pressure to be The Source Of All the Answers, it became a place where we shared stories, learned, and discovered together. My willingness to journey through my not knowing as I prepared for (and lead) class, equipped me to help my students journey through their not knowing. And isn't that what learning is? The journey of moving from not knowing toward discovery?

I don't have all the answers, and I don't expect you to either.

A number of my students were quite startled to hear this admission coming out of my mouth, some pleasantly so and many skeptically so. I'm pretty sure none of them believed me in the beginning.

I know it's working when students begin asking the same questions that I ask them as they reason through their own thinking instead of looking to me to provide a conclusory response. This tells me that *learning* is happening in my classrooms: when students respond to the space created for their thoughts by occupying it and filling it with their own capable, independent thinking.

Your Turn

Exploring I Don't Know

*Grab something to write with and your **Brave Educator Action Pack** (get your free download at krystlecobran.com/the-brave-educator).*

Carve out 15 minutes. Think about the following questions and write your responses down:

◆ Do you feel the pressure to know everything as you lead classroom discussions about race in your classroom?

◆ If so, how does this pressure affect the learning environment?

◆ How do you think your classroom environment would shift if you embraced the power of "I Don't Know?"

◆ What makes you most uncomfortable about the prospect of telling your students when you don't know something, or that you need to do some research because you don't have an immediate response to a question they pose or concern they raise?

Yes, this is risky. But the payoff is worth it. As educators, we possess an unusual degree of influence over our students. Consistently demonstrating that learning is a shared process, and conveying our confidence in our students' capability by making room for their growth instead of dominating the room with our insecurity and fear helps set everyone free to walk through the learning process.

Your Turn

A Few Quick "I Don't Know" Variations

◆ Variations on "I Don't Know" that may work for you:
  – "Great question, I'd like to think some more about that. Can I get back to you by/in _____ [insert time period]?"

> - "I've never thought of it that way. I'd like to take some time to go over that. Could you come see me after class so we can talk some more about your perspective?"
> - "That's a really innovative approach. I'd like to consider it some more before I respond. Could I get back to you _____ [insert time period here]?"

Three little words, *I Don't Know*, changed everything in my classroom. These words reduce the pressure we as educators feel to be The Source of All the Answers, and help us show up in the classroom as ourselves. Since we're the models, tone-setters, and primary decision-makers in our classrooms, our choice to do this directly sheds light on the learning path for the students we serve.

 Make Tiny Tweaks

Release the Pressure to Have All the Answers

Having to have all the answers all the time is like living with a leech. It drains our energy, sucks the motivation right out of us. Not knowing isn't failure. *Not knowing is where discovery begins.* I know we've talked about this in earlier sections, but it's worth repeating. Because, sometimes, we get so afraid our students will ask something we don't know the answer to that we start avoiding engaging with our students before we even know exactly what we're trying to avoid. Let the pressure go. You have research skills. You have communication skills. You have access to books, fact-based, peer-reviewed research, and well-researched articles and resources. You are capable. You can find your way to the information you need. Turn it into an adventure. Give yourself permission to discover. As you do, you'll give your students permission to do the same.

Step 2

How to Decide What Really Matters in Your Classroom

Pay Attention If You're Feeling Overwhelmed

I started teaching four weeks after delivering my second child. (There are tiny humans in my house born 14.5 months apart.) Figuring out what was important to me in my classroom wasn't something I could afford to take lightly. I was responsible for building a course called Race & the Law from scratch, and to say I was tight on time is a dramatic understatement. Once I knew that I didn't know exactly how to start, and I felt the pressure of expecting myself to be perfect begin to climb, I knew I had to make some major shifts in my approach. Otherwise, I'd stay stuck in a sludge of fear and do nothing. Or I'd take the pressure I was feeling and dump it on my students in an attempt to hide just how overwhelmed I was feeling.

Neither option appealed to me.

I didn't know exactly where I was going, and I knew it. I struggled. But as I wrestled, it occurred to me that I hadn't given myself permission to *decide what really mattered to me in my classroom*. Either I was going to fake it, or I was going to start with what I did know, find my way, and build from there. Skipping ahead to figuring out course content without first identifying my course goals increased my frustration and deprived me of clarity. It wasn't important for me to know every single word I'd speak every single day I taught. It *was* important for me to identify some Foundational Goals that could guide us as we moved through the material.

The Power of Deciding What You Value

There were four Foundational Goals that were absolutely essential. (Please note: I am fleshing these out in retrospect and grouping them into categories for clarity and usefulness. This is not an exhaustive list, and this process did not feel remotely as clear or concise as I was discovering which strategies and tools worked in my classroom. Let your own process be what it is. Clarity will come as you move through the journey.)

Foundational Goal 1

Help Students Think for Themselves (i.e., Become Critical Thinkers)

I had no interest in creating tiny clones of my brain. The world isn't the easiest place to navigate, and experience taught me that it's harder, not easier, when we spend our lives trying to think the way we're supposed to think, and do what we think we're supposed to do instead of doing the hard work of understanding how we actually think so we can decide what we actually want to do. I wanted my students to move forward in life with tools that foster their own thinking. I wanted them to (at least begin to) recognize their inherent capability to use their own brain, problem-solve, and make their own choices. I wanted them to ask hard questions. I wanted my classroom to be a place where my students could practice learning how to think for themselves.

Foundational Goal 2

Teach Students How to Talk About Race With People Who Don't Think Like They Think

I wanted my classroom to be conversation-driven, not lecture-focused. I did not want the only voice my students heard to be my voice. Which meant I couldn't be the center of attention. I needed to figure out how to create a dynamic environment where I equipped students for classroom conversations about race without excluding any student based on their perspective or experience(s) and somehow empower them to go beyond talking with me to begin having productive conversations with each other.

Foundational Goal 3

Establish and Preserve Mutual Dignity and Respect, While Creating Shared Learning Experiences

If I was going to ask my students to do the first two things (see Goals 1 and 2 immediately before this one), then I had to find a way to establish and preserve mutual dignity and respect, while creating shared learning. Without the safety of mutual dignity and mutual respect, classroom conversations about race devolve into combat and competition; an energy-draining scene where the person with the greatest ability to talk at the other(s) "wins" (see our conversation about combatation in the Preface). This scenario is ripe for defensiveness, judgment, disconnection, and looping frustration, none of which facilitates consistent connection or learning.

Foundational Goal 4

Effectively Design and Cover Course Content

All these goals existed within the context of a semester-long course. That meant that the course materials I selected, the way I arranged them in the syllabus, and the way I chose to cover topics in class all needed to work together to support my Foundational Goals. I had the flexibility to make shifts as I needed to, but I did need to make some decisions about how and when to contextualize and focus the material we were covering so that students were equipped and empowered to handle challenging conversations in advance. There's no point in attempting to lead productive classroom conversation about race without context. (Course content provides context.) Otherwise, I and/or my personal experiences become the context, and that simply doesn't line up with Goals 1 through 3.

Countless decisions about how to lead classroom conversations about race sprang from these four Foundational Goals. For example, I needed to make a decision about my teaching style. *Was I going to lecture each day or did I want to teach in a way that felt more interactive?* I decided to teach by asking questions. *Why?* Because it was a flexible format that was responsive to student needs and supported my goal of teaching my students to think for themselves. *How did I ask questions? Did I treat students to a hefty dose of the Socratic method I endured during law school?* Hard no. *Why?* Because I will never forget the day I messed up getting the right class reading done, and I felt like crawling into a deep, dark pit.

The shame I felt is difficult to overstate. (There are tears in my eyes as I write this to you.) Risking the possibility of putting my students in a similar position didn't line up with Goals 1, 2, or 3. *How did I teach by asking questions?* I chose a conversational format that went something like this: I'd ask a question directly connected to the material we were covering. Then I'd listen to the response of the student(s) who volunteered to share their perspective. Based on student responses, we'd engage in conversation and then I'd ask another question, essentially pulling from students' contributions and our dialogue to establish the core components of each lesson and then using relevant contributions to build momentum and shape the direction of our dialogue. This interactive approach supported all four Foundational Goals. Teaching by asking questions was an extremely important decision for me. But I don't know that I would have made that choice if I hadn't had some clarity around my core priorities. Teaching by asking questions wasn't one of my four Foundational Goals, but it became an Essential Factor because it directly supported the achievement of my Foundational Goals.

 Share Your Story

What are some Foundational Goals that help shape your classroom conversations about race? Visit krystlecobran.com/the-brave-educator to share them with me.

Additional Essential Factors in my classroom included listening to and asking for feedback so that I could rapidly make adjustments, incorporating conversations about current events so that the course content felt current and relevant, building in flexibility in my course schedule for in-class conversations so students had time to process the material we were covering (see our discussion about Shared Story Blocks in Section III) and I could identify areas where content wasn't sufficiently clear, and being intentional about connecting the dots between each chunk of material we covered in the course so that (as much as humanly possible) students continued to have conversations in context.

Making the choice to decide what your priorities are in classroom conversations about race can save you a great deal of time, reduce frustration, and provide clarity when the way forward seems invisible. Foundational Goals become touchstones in awkward situations, guides in fun conversations that start to wander, and motivation to help you generate forward momentum when you get stuck. Each of my Foundational Goals means a great deal to me at both a professional and personal level.

I'll write them one more time for you, but this time, I'll limit myself to a few sentences about why they matter so much to me at a personal level.

Foundational Goal 1

Help Students Think for Themselves (i.e., Become Critical Thinkers)

I spent a lot of time as a student sitting in classrooms thinking something was wrong with me, believing something was wrong with my brain because I didn't want to think inside of a box. There's nothing wrong with my brain. It needs to be supported, respected, and challenged so it can absorb, create, adapt, and grow. If I can save my students the agony of believing there's something wrong with thinking outside the box, I'll spare them a lot of agony and get them further down the road of embracing their unique capability.

Foundational Goal 2

Teach Students How to Talk About Race With People
Who Don't Think Like They Think

There are no two people who think and feel the same way about everything all the time. Yet, we often have the expectation that we have to completely agree before we can connect. So, especially in difficult conversations, we end up pretending, staying quiet, or going along because we believe it's what we have to do to get along. Instead of building connection, this creates tension, avoidance, and division. I want my students to understand that shared humanity isn't dependent on complete agreement. I want them to feel what it's like to respect someone and disagree with them *at the same time*. I think that could change the world.

Foundational Goal 3

Establish and Preserve Mutual Dignity and Respect, While Creating Shared Learning Experiences

Every student sitting in my classroom is a leader somewhere for someone. Every single one. Because even if they're not at the head of a group, they're responsible for leading themselves. So I want them to feel what it's like to be in that trusted role. To understand that leadership and trying to control people so that they think like we think aren't the same thing. It's important to me that they understand that their words, their perspective, and their contribution to the conversation have a real impact on our classroom environment.

Foundational Goal 4

Effectively Design and Cover Course Content (See Goals 1–3)

I hate being bored. Or perpetually confused.

Each Foundational Goal was rooted in deep professional and personal values. I needed those roots to identify the Essential Factors that supported my Foundational Goals and to get me through the general unpredictability that comes with leading classroom conversations about race. Without the deeply rooted reasons that shaped my Foundational Goals, I don't know if I would have endured this process. And I certainly don't know how I would have made sure that each tiny step we took was pointed toward a productive big-picture end goal.

Crucial Tip
Decide what you value in the classroom so you can create valuable classroom experiences.

Maybe you teach extremely young students. Perhaps your students aren't quite so tiny anymore. Either way, you have the power to shape how conversations about race work in your classroom. Identifying your Foundational Goals can help you feel more prepared and less overwhelmed.

Your Turn

Let's Identify Your Foundational Goals

*Grab something to write with and your **Brave Educator Action Pack** (get your free download at krystlecobran.com/the-brave-educator).*

Take your time and work through this exercise when you have an extended moment to think.

1. What really matters to you as an educator when it comes to leading conversations about race in your classroom?

    I want conversations in my classroom to _____ [fill in the blank].

    Write as much as you'd like, and be sure to respond to this prompt at least four times. Feel free to respond more than four times if you need to keep going.

2. Now summarize each response into a heading. For example, if you wrote "I really want my students to be exposed to diverse stories," then your heading might be "Exposing my students to diverse stories."

3. Make a list of your headings. These are your Foundational Goals.

4. Write what really matters to you personally and professionally about each heading you've summarized directly underneath it.

5. Take a moment to review what matters to you professionally and personally.

6. How will these Foundational Goals effect the way you lead classroom conversations about race?

    Make a list.

7. Which of these effects are essential and highly beneficial?

    Make a list.

8. Why are these effects essential and highly beneficial?

    Because _____ [fill in the blank with an effect]
    creates _____ [discuss what the effect creates

here] and that benefits my students by _____ _____ [describe the benefit to your students here].

9. Fill in the prompt below after taking 10–15 minutes to review your responses above.

10. I choose to prioritize _____ [insert important choice about effects here] in order to create _____ [insert benefit to students in classroom environment here]. Repeat. The important choices you list in the first blank are your Essential Factors.

Well done. You've just made a list of your Foundational Goals and your Essential Factors. You have clarity around what your priorities are when race comes up in your classroom. You can always update or adjust your Foundational Goals or Essential Factors based on your classroom needs or the feedback you receive. This is not a limiting container. Be flexible. Be honest with yourself about what's working and what's not. Notice if any of your Foundational Goals are getting in the way of student learning, and shift quickly. *Keep being honest with yourself, especially if you're feeling frustrated or overwhelmed.* If something's not working, it's not working. If something's not productive, it's not productive. This isn't information to be ashamed of; it's a precious data point that will help you carve a new direction.

Here are a few things to avoid in your Foundational Goals and Essential Factors:

1. Anything that sounds like fixing people (e.g., getting students to align themselves specifically with your point of view).

2. Anything that makes you omnipotent. If you must transform yourself into an all-knowing being to achieve it, it's probably way more about serving your ego than it is about serving your students.

3. Anything that's passive-aggressive and manipulative (see Item 1 in this list).

4. Anything that turns students into stereotypes (e.g., deciding to only let people from marginalized/majority groups be part of the conversation so that they can educate all the other less privileged/more privileged people).

5. Anything that rests in cultural preferences, presumptions, or assumptions about how people are supposed to be and how people are supposed to think (e.g., requiring students to ignore art, history, music, or pop culture in classroom conversations about race).

6. Pretending that everyone's lived experience is approximately the same (e.g., denying any student's reality in any way, shape, or form).

Make them simple. Meaningful. Doable. And challenging. Design them, above all else, to facilitate learning for your students as you learn how to navigate conversations about race in the classroom. Hopefully, taking the time to discover what really matters in your classroom(s) will position you to generate value for your students that lasts long after the conversation has ended.

 Make Tiny Tweaks

Create Priorities That are Grounded in Real Experiences

We teach our students how to learn when we're open to learning ourselves. Being honest about what we don't know and letting go of pretense isn't easy. But it has the power to take our conversations about race away from being disconnected and draining toward becoming opportunities for connection and collaborative learning. So when you're caught by surprise, what you need most isn't to start pulling answers from thin air. Instead, reach for priorities that really matter. Draw on your Foundational Goals to respond in ways that open unexpected Paths of Discovery.

Step 3

Create Boundaries That Support You and Your Students in the Classroom

Boundaries Are Important in Conversations About Race

Race is a massive, layered, and complex topic. (Exceedingly so.) Leaping into classroom dialogue about race without identifying clear boundaries is like trying to cross the Grand Canyon, on foot, in 30 minutes, with no water. Not going to happen. We need to establish our Terms of Engagement.

Here's the thing: We don't have many mutually agreed upon cultural guidelines to help us through navigating conversations about race in the classroom. We haven't yet figured out how to talk with each other about what the guidelines should be outside of school walls. As a result, conversations about race can feel a bit like a highly confusing pick-your-own-adventure game (where everyone might not quite be playing the same game). In the absence of broadly shared cultural boundaries around how we talk about race, the shared boundaries that exist inside of our classrooms are likely going to be boundaries that we (educators) establish. Classrooms are one of the few spaces that exist where people from varied racial and ethnic groups can learn how to talk *with* each other about *what the experience of race feels like*: a place where history, science, sociology, current events, politics, economics, culture, etc. (i.e., macro/big-picture/systemic issues) intersect with personal stories. The classroom is a Cultural Connection Point; a place where human beings can learn how to talk about race with people who may not think about or experience race like they do. This puts educators at the epicenter of shaping cultural norms around conversations about race.

I don't say this to put more pressure on you. No one needs that. I say this so that you are aware that you have power to influence how we talk about race as a culture *because* you are an educator. Your perspective, your curiosity, your willingness to embrace the not-knowingness of it all has the power to impact the perspective, approach, and cultivation of critical thinking in the students you lead.

No One Is Coming to Class Because They Want Us to Impress Them With Our Brilliance

Early on, I made the mistake of teaching from a place of defensiveness because I felt so much pressure to have all of the answers. I spent a lot of time thinking about all the ways I wasn't cut out to walk my students through the race conversation. But my students weren't coming to class because they wanted to watch me prove my brilliance. Educational achievement in my classroom wasn't centered on students' discovering how I—on my own and without help from another human being ever—had somehow self-generated the perfect set of (miracle) solutions that permanently and irrevocably transformed race conversations forever. Nope. My students came to class because they wanted to learn.

They were hoping to discover. They showed up trusting that I would carve out boundaries to support listening and connection rather than attacking and picking sides, without creating so many Terms of Engagement that it became impossible to have a real conversation. It was up to me to identify which boundaries were nonnegotiable.

LEARNING HOW TO LISTEN

SHARED DISCOVERY

CONNECTING TO UNFAMILIAR STORIES

MUTUAL RESPECT

Your Turn

Are You Feeling Defensive?

*Grab something to write with and your **Brave Educator Action Pack** (get your free download at krystlecobran.com/the-brave-educator).*

Follow these steps:

1. Take a deep breath.
2. I see you. You're already feeling defensive.
3. I hope you're laughing now.
4. Answer the following prompt: When race comes up in my classroom(s) I feel defensive about _____ [fill in the blank].

> 5. Now, let's get curious.
> 6. Stay curious and do a Defensiveness Flip by completing this prompt:
>
> Today I choose to feel less worried about _____
> [list the thing(s) you're feeling defensive about here] because
> I'm going to _____ [list the positive and simple(!)
> action step you're going to take here] so I can learn more about
> _____ [repeat the thing you're feeling defensive
> about here].

My having all the answers was not at all a nonnegotiable Term of Engagement. It was, in reality a gigantic hindrance to the work of facilitating genuine classroom conversations about race that help students think for themselves.

Mutual respect, on the other hand, was nonnegotiable. Attempting to engage in meaningful conversation about race without establishing and preserving mutual respect is like trying to sleep on a boat in the middle of a hurricane—not feasible, and someone is likely to get severely harmed in the process.

Mutual discovery was nonnegotiable. No one in the room is expected to have all the answers—about anything, including what their own personal experience of race is like, and especially not about what the experience of race is like for people who look like they do. There are no explainers in my classroom(s).

Listening was nonnegotiable. (There were opportunities for debate built into my course schedule(s), but even our debates were designed to be more dialogue-driven than prove-a-point-driven.) My choice to teach primarily by asking questions rather than by lecturing (see the discussion about Foundational Goals and Essential Factors in Step 2) had the impact of generating listening and conversation on multiple levels—between myself and my students, among my students, and within individual students as they learned how to listen to and examine their own thought processes.

Your Turn

Let's Start Exploring Your Terms of Engagement

*Grab something to write with and your **Brave Educator Action Pack** (get your free download at krystlecobran.com/the-brave-educator).*

Find a quiet place to do this exercise.

Pretend you're a student in your classroom. You're sitting behind a desk, looking up at you (the teacher) during a conversation about race.

Answer the following questions from the perspective of your students:

1. What do you need? Make a list of at least two to three needs.
2. What are you most concerned about? Make a list of at least two to three concerns.
3. What do you want to talk about? Make a list of at least two to three topics related to race.
4. How would you like the teacher (you) to guide the conversation? Make a list of at least two to three ways you'd like to feel as a student in this conversation.
5. What do you need to feel like you belong in the conversation? Make a list of at least two to three descriptive characteristics.
6. What support do you need from your teacher if the conversation goes sideways? Make a list of at least two to three needs.
7. What would you need from your teacher and the conversation to stay engaged and actively participate? Make a list of two to three needs.

You're you again.

Take a moment to review what you've written.

Now, as the educator responsible for navigating conversations about race in your classroom, what have you written down that is absolutely essential? What is vital to having classroom conversations about race that facilitate student learning, growth, and discovery?

Make a list.

Here are examples of prompts you can use to make your list:

In race conversations in my classroom(s), we treat each other with _____.

In race conversations in my classroom(s), I (the educator) prioritize _____.

In race conversations in my classroom(s), we focus our dialogue on _____.

In race conversations in my classroom (s), we create

_____.

This list is the core of your Terms of Engagement.

Implementing these Terms of Engagement directly supported my Foundational Goals. Students began judging each other less and listening more, even when they disagreed. They began communicating more clearly as they reached for connection and understanding over agreement. The dialogue in the classroom became more open and free-flowing. Students began sharing more than their analyses of the material we were covering; they began to share how their life experiences intertwined with the material we were covering. Students began to talk about perspectives other than their own from a place of engagement rather than defensiveness.

I know it sounds simple. But when it comes to navigating conversations about race in the classroom, we often skip straight over simple because we're worried our strategies aren't good enough unless they are next to impossible to attain. It's not true. Leading conversations about race that work in the classroom doesn't start with walking through the door, guard up, equipped with overly complex strategies to lead an already complex conversation and a point to prove. When we bring meaningful goals (Foundational Goals), intentional choices (Essential Factors), and clear boundaries (Terms of Engagement) to the table, we begin to carve out spaces for conversations about race in the classroom where there's room for learning, and listening to multiple points of view.

 Make Tiny Tweaks

Get and Stay Grounded

Your Foundational Goals, Essential Factors, and Terms of Engagement are vital stops on your road map. It takes time and energy to identify the priorities that fit student needs in your specific classroom(s), but it's work that can save you a great deal of frustration and help you avoid missteps. Conversations about race that productively facilitate learning and discovery don't just happen. Use these tools to create boundaries that support learning in your classroom. Pay attention to what's working, and notice what's not. Listen to student feedback. If you need to shift your boundaries, do it in a way that supports your Foundational Goals. Remember that you're not figuring this out in a vacuum. That's good news.

Step 4

We All Have This. Pay Attention to Yours

Let's Get Personal

I caught a look from one student to another. The Look came from one of my most precocious and bright students, right after I made an encouraging remark toward a student who happens to look like I do. Our eyes connected, and this student (who I deeply respect and believe is extraordinary) quickly looked away in embarrassment. I kept teaching, but internally, I felt a tidal wave of emotions:

> *Did this student think that I was biased toward people who share my racial background?*
> *Am I biased toward students who share my racial background?*
> *Have I been unwittingly letting down students who don't share my racial background?*
> *Am I showing signs of preference?*
> *Am I failing?*
> *Am I being more encouraging toward certain students than others?*

We never had a direct conversation about this, but the silent exchange stayed with me. It remains with me to this day.

In the immediate aftermath I felt like my options (in oversimplified terms) pointed in two directions. Either I could dismiss this student outright and go about the business of attempting to prove that I was fair and righteous in every way at every moment (this doesn't at all sound like an extreme response), or I could attempt (for just a moment) to see my classroom from this student's perspective in an effort to empathize with what this student might be feeling or perceiving.

I'll admit it. I struggled. I felt hurt. I felt judged. I put a great deal of work into creating a classroom environment that generates belonging, connection, mutual dignity, and respect for every single student present. It was a terrifying endeavor to do any of this, and I was scared every single day I stepped into the classroom to embark down very unfamiliar paths with extremely high stakes at play. Defensiveness was the easiest thing to reach for.

I wanted to prove that I was fair. I wanted to make a point about how hard I was working. I felt like I needed to show this student just how much work I put into creating a fair and safe classroom environment. I was very, very triggered. Very triggered. We all have stuff around leading conversations about race in the classroom, and this interaction brought mine straight to the surface.

I didn't want to see any of this in myself, but the truth is that I needed to know. I needed to know that this student might be concerned that I'd evaluate them less favorably because they didn't look like me. I needed to know that this student was worried. I needed to know that this student needed reassurance that I wasn't going to dismiss their perspective, their opinion, their performance, or their contributions. I needed to know that the subject matter we were covering was so delicate for this student that they may have needed a bit more encouragement than they'd received thus far in order to continue to engage and endure. I needed to begin understanding the degree of power that my demeanor and my words carried in that classroom—even words of encouragement meant to keep the dialogue moving forward.

And I needed to understand that inside of myself, I was on pins and needles because I felt defensive and deeply sensitive about all of it.

All of this left me with a choice to make about how to respond.

When Feelings Come Up, Take a Look

Being this triggered was an invitation to reach for connection. It wasn't a signal to embrace avoidance, defensiveness, or deflecting as methods of coping in the classroom. Feeling triggered also wasn't a sign that I needed to dismiss this student, write them off, and point to the extensive list of sacrifices I'd made and ways I'd gone above and beyond to create a safe and inclusive classroom environment.

Being this triggered was a call to take some time to deal with my stuff. Whether I wanted to or not. Even though this wasn't an invitation I particularly wanted to receive, the other option didn't at all line up with my Foundational Goals, Essential Factors, or Terms of Engagement.

So I took a look. And I'm still taking a look, to be honest. (There's a lot to see.) One shift I made in the immediate aftermath (starting with that very class) was making a mental note to do my best to ensure that I was encouraging all of my students. Yes, I thought I was being generous and inclusive with my encouragement before The Look happened, but that's beyond the point. I was now conscious that I might need to be more aware of my choices. I kept practicing this habit in future classes. (Over time, I continued to shift my approach. Encouragement that served the function of fueling both individual students and the classroom discussion became one of my larger, overarching Essential Factors (see the dialogue on Foundational Goals and Essential Factors in Step 2.))

This student and I ended up remaining in contact after the course ended. I never brought up The Look. Neither did the student. To be frank, there's no need for either of us to bring it up because that look, along with all the triggering emotions that accompanied it, *was extremely valuable information that I needed to have*. Information that helped me tweak how I lead conversations about race to this day.

Why am I revealing this not-very-lovely-to-behold moment to you? (I'm asking myself this very question. *Why, Krystle, why?*)

Crucial Tip
It takes strength and courage to ask for help.

Conversations about race can be extremely triggering. Since I am not a trained psychologist, I make no bones about practicing very serious and clear boundaries when nearing or approaching the trauma realm with my students, my clients, and my community (readers, viewers, etc.). I take this seriously. I strongly encourage fellow humans seeking tools for processing or navigating challenging life experiences to find an outstanding and healthy therapist to get the support you need.

So, at this moment in *The Brave Educator*, please hear me: Seek appropriately trained support if reading these words brings emotions or experiences to the surface that feel completely overwhelming and/or debilitating.

Since most conversations about race are actually combat in disguise, many of us do our best to avoid conversations about race, and cross-cultural conversations about race in particular. We treat it like the plague. Even if we ourselves haven't been involved in, dismissed, or silenced in a publicly humiliating "conversation" about race, the pain of being forgotten, screamed over, judged, ignored, or labeled can feel so overwhelming that avoidance looks like the only rational option.

Frequently, public conversations about race happen in an eruption after someone says something horribly ill-informed, inappropriate, discriminatory, and hurtful. Usually, the cycle goes something like this. Public Figure says something horrific, insulting, insensitive, dismissive, or ill-timed about race. Members of the public (Public) experience volcanic response. Public Figure says they are not a racist. Public says that saying that you're not a racist makes you a racist. Public Figure is freaked out and either disappears or starts digging in their heels. Public splits into camps. Camp 1: Public Figure is not a racist. They just made a mistake. Camp 2 needs to calm down. Camp 2: Public Figure is a racist. They said what they really thought based on how they really feel. Camp 1 needs to understand that these racist words hurt real people who have endured and continue to endure real suffering in real life and who have real feelings. Public Figure is publicly punished in some way. They lose a position, opportunity, status, money, visibility, or some other valuable thing. Public Figure semi-disappears from view. Public remains divided into Camp 1 and Camp 2. Volcanic eruption calms down until the next time another Public Figure says something horribly ill-informed, inappropriate, discriminatory, and hurtful. Neither Public Figure, Public Camp 1, nor Public Camp 2 has learned anything about how to have meaningful conversations about race with each other. No one feels understood. No one knows what needs to happen to create change for the better. Everyone retreats to their separate corners with people who think and feel like they do to gripe about how little "those people" understand them.

There is literally no conversation in this conversation.

There is screaming. There is labeling. There is combat. There is judgment. There is (sometimes) punishment. There is disagreement. There is pain. There is disgust. There is disappointment. There is talking past, around, and at.

There is very little talking *with*. There is almost no connection with viewpoints that are different from our own. There is almost no real listening, certainly not listening that leads to shared understanding. There is no cultivation of shared belonging, connection, mutual respect, or dignity across categories. There seems to be a general conclusion before the conversation even begins that this is how the race conversation has been, this is how the race conversation is going to be, and since nothing is going to change, we might as well do our darnedest to make sure we get our point across. We enter conversations about race with arms up, verbal weapons drawn, ears closed, and judgments made. We talk at, past, and around each other. This is not conversation. This is combat—combatation. It's difficult to watch and intimidating to even think about diving into after watching or experiencing this cycle repeatedly. This setup literally eats teachable moments alive. It devours our motivation as educators to wander into (what seems to be) the forbidden territory of race conversations. I mean, really, who actually wants to risk leading a conversation about race in the classroom when clearly there are approximately 10 million that can go wrong in an instant?

Crucial Tip
Talking at each other is not the same as talking with each other.

Remember The Look I was telling you about a few pages ago? Let's go back to that moment for a second. I could have stopped the class and attempted to engage in a "conversation" about that look with that student right then and there. I could have used my platform to "hold that student accountable" for The Look while driving home the point to my students that I was the one in charge of the classroom environment and therefore deserving of unconditional deference and respect. (Whew. That sentence makes me shudder.) Not one person in the room would benefit from this approach. In no way does this promote open conversation or learning. What was required in that moment wasn't an external conversation with the student. What I needed was an internal conversation with myself.

I needed to look at my own stuff. Any productive external response to awkward moments in conversations about race in the classroom is directly influenced by the conversations I choose to have (or avoid) within myself. Taking a look at what was bothering me most, not outward combat in reaction to what I observed, was the response that had the most potential to increase learning. Looking at my own stuff helped me see things I couldn't see before, so I could begin to identify where I needed to Make Tiny Tweaks or adjust my Foundational Goals, Essential Factors, and Terms of Engagement.

I was the one who was triggered. I was the one who was concerned. I was the one who was worried I was missing something or communicating something I didn't intend to communicate. It's not my students' responsibility to address those needs for me. It's my responsibility to carve out space (i.e., on my commute, on the walk back to my car, while taking a shower or drinking that warm cup of tea) to process, to feel, and to be with my own stuff so that I don't let that Gigantic Bag of My Stuff that has Nothing to Do With You block learning and development in the classroom.

What does all this have to do with how you lead classroom conversations about race?

Because the societal template for how we publicly talk about race leaves very little room for actual conversation, and our default position when we're not sure what to do next seems to be to defend whatever stance we've settled on, it's highly unlikely that we'll be able to figure out how to create a classroom environment that facilitates conversation (not combat) about race unless we're willing to begin by learning how to navigate this conversation *within ourselves*.

So here's what we're going to do: We're going to start conversations about race with ourselves in the ways we want to start conversations about race in the classroom. We're going to move through a conversation about race with ourselves in the way we want to move through a conversation about race in the classroom. We're going to set a goal for what we want to take away from these conversations about race with ourselves and keep that goal in mind as we move through our internal dialogue. We're going to decide what we want to learn as we engage in conversations about race with ourselves and allow that to guide us away from beating up on ourselves for what we don't know as we choose instead move toward learning and discovery. We're going to decide what our main goals are during conversations about race with ourselves and let those goals guide us through.

Yep. We're going to do this. No matter how corny, strange, or weird it sounds. Would you like to know why we're going to do this? *Because it's incredibly difficult to give to our students what we refuse to give ourselves.* And it's going to be really hard to help students engage in conversation and not combat if we as leaders in the classroom aren't willing to get curious about our internal dialogue.

We're also going to do this because the classroom isn't where we go to process our stuff. And we've all got stuff. We need to know where our tender places are. We need to begin discovering what we feel most defensive or fearful about in conversations about race. We need to discover where we're defaulting to blame, finger-pointing, distancing, or deflection because there's something sticky we're trying to step around. We need to learn how to practice taking care of ourselves in conversations about race so that we can cultivate the bandwidth we need to tend to stay responsive to our students when race comes up in the classroom.

Crucial Tip
It's hard to give to our students what we refuse to give to ourselves.

We need to get familiar with our stuff so that we can show up in the classroom prepared to navigate the unexpected. We can't work through our stuff when we're pretending it isn't there.

This may be the most difficult part of leading conversations about race in the classroom. Without fail, it triggers awareness of our own baggage. Whether it's the degree to which we are (or are) not prepared to lead discussions, past discussions that went sideways, or coping with our own rapidly expanding awareness as students open up and share personal stories, perspectives, and experiences, it is imperative to be aware that leading conversations about race in the classroom will inevitably bring up our own personal stuff and to have a plan for how we will proactively respond and cope in advance.

Your Turn

Give Yourself Some Support
*Grab something to write with and your **Brave Educator Action Pack** (get your free download at krystlecobran.com/the-brave-educator).*

Imagine what it would feel like to be truly supported in your classroom during conversations about race. (Let's focus on supporting you right now.)

Give yourself permission to really think about this and be really honest with yourself.

Answer the following questions:

1. What resources would you want on hand?
2. What words of encouragement would be spoken?
3. What boundaries would be set (time, tone, subject matter, degree of student engagement, ways of shifting the conversation, etc.)?
4. Now, what one thing would make bring you the greatest degree of relief in the classroom?
5. How can you begin giving yourself just a little bit of the support you need?

   For example, if you need to hear, "I know this feels overwhelming in the face of creating multiple lesson plans and managing curricula requirements day in and day out. I respect your courage. I am here to support you." Then write that down somewhere you'll see it throughout the day—a sticky note on your desk, a note in your planner, stuck to the bottom of your chair so you see it every time you sit down.

Build putting fuel into your tank into everyday moments so that when you need to navigate challenging conversations you can do it from a place of feeling seen and supported.

Take the time to feel. (Even if it's two minutes.) It's worth it.

Doing this work might feel strange, but it's worth it. By working through conversations about race with ourselves we're building the bandwidth we need to deal with live real-time questions, discussions, and challenges that come up in conversations about race in the classroom. Taking care of ourselves is part of what helps us respond with conscious intention instead of passive reaction.

Make Tiny Tweaks

Where We Struggle Is Where We Need the Most Care

Taking the time to think about where we struggle in conversations about race isn't frivolous. It's necessary. It's us taking the time to give ourselves the same respect, dignity, and listening we want to give to our students. So much of education often feels like it's about serving the needs of everyone but educators. This book exists to serve you as you serve others. Know that you're not the only one who feels triggered or defensive or who struggles with navigating conversations about race in the classroom. You don't have to know how to deal with every single possible challenge that might come up. Start by giving yourself the support you need so that you can show up for yourself and your students.

Section III

Seven Connection Strategies to Help You Navigate Classroom Conversations About Race

Connection Strategy 1

A Quick Chat About Uncomfortable Moments in the Classroom

When Things Get Uncomfortable

I'll never forget this exchange. As I remember it, a determined yet exasperated hand flew up into the air. This student was outstanding. Consistently prepared, willing to ask hard questions, committed to the learning process. On this particular day, this student was frustrated. Validly so. We'd been moving through a great deal of classroom material and some larger themes were beginning to evolve. Patterns were appearing—sociopolitical and judicial (our classroom material relied heavily on Supreme Court cases). As we got deeper into the course, students were moving from one level of awareness to another. They were growing, thinking independently. They began sharing personal experiences connected with the material. My classes inevitably involve a degree of sitting with the gray (that's the nature of constitutional law) and leaving room for students to think their own thoughts.

It was an uncomfortable kind of day. As I listened to this student's question, I understood what they were looking for. Simplicity. Clarity. Solutions. Conclusions. Concise remedies and step-by-step recipes for how to fix issues around race that have existed for centuries. We've all felt this. But my job as a teacher isn't to make the race conversation simple. It's to carve out space for real classroom conversation with each other (not at each other) as we move through the material. I'm there to facilitate learning. So I listened to this student, engaged the difficult questions they shared, paused to validate the frustration this student verbalized, attempted to connect our exploration to the classroom dialogue that day, and gave this student permission to sit with their feelings without letting my reaction to their feelings shape the entirety of our class discussion.

Being in an academic environment doesn't make feelings go away. My students needed space to process their emotions and feelings just as much as they needed me to teach the material. My job was to teach. Not fix. Which meant that my students' feelings weren't a problem. They were part of the process. And the deeper we got into the material, the more I began to notice that the expression of shared feeling is absolutely essential in creating meaningful classroom conversations about race.

Release Control, Embrace Learning

Sometimes, as we attempt to dive into a difficult classroom conversation, we (educators) default to thinking that we need to "take control" of the dialogue, let students know "who's in charge," and make sure we "prove the point we need to prove." But getting through uncomfortable classroom conversations doesn't require trying to control what our students think.

It requires engaging with what our students share.

Sometimes, what our students share is how they're struggling—with the material, with larger societal realities, with the lack of clear answers and the absence of simple solutions, with the stress that comes with growing awareness and deeper understanding.

Crucial Tip
Engage with what students share.

It's not our responsibility to fix feelings—anyone's feelings. We witness feelings, respond to feelings, and experience feelings. Educators aren't fixers. We can create boundaries to help everyone in our classroom learn how to respond to feelings in healthy ways. We can make room for feelings and self-expression in the learning process. We can acknowledge feelings and treat them with dignity and respect. We don't fix them. We don't pretend they're not there. We don't ignore them, bury them, or brush by them. Feelings and learning aren't archenemies. Responding responsibly to the feelings we find pleasant and the ones that are more difficult to deal with without spewing them all over each other, without turning our feelings into an excuse to avoid the challenging parts of the learning process, is a skill—one that takes time and practice to learn.

Crucial Tip
Give yourself and your students permission to feel.

Three Simple Tools You Can Use to Help Students Process Their Own Emotions in the Learning Process

Listen Well

The first tool is just Listening. Listening plays many roles in the classroom. In addition to helping us understand the precise support students need, creating space for students to more clearly recognize their own capability, and helping us explore new ideas and perspectives in the classroom, Listening helps us give students the room they need to acknowledge their own emotions, without putting us in the role of fixer.

Your Turn

 What Does Listening Look Like in Your Classroom?
Grab something to write with and your **Brave Educator Action Pack** (get your free download at krystlecobran.com/the-brave-educator).

No one knows your classroom like you do. Take five minutes to explore what listening looks like for you and your students.

Answer these questions:

1. How can I clearly communicate to my students that I am listening to them? *Write two to three concrete steps you can take.*
2. How will clearly communicating to students that I'm listening benefit student learning? *Write any benefits for your specific students that come to mind. Aim for at least two to three.*

Here are five simple examples of what listening might look like for you:

Pause briefly before responding.
Look students in the eye.
Positive feedback (e.g., *I'm listening . . ., Keep going . . .*).
Encourage internal reflection (e.g., *How do you feel about that?*).
Help students connect the dots between their feelings and the material (e.g., *Let's think about _____ [what student just said/asked]. How does that connect to our conversation about _____ [identify relevant course content here]?*).

Listening establishes that our classrooms are places where students don't have to show up with the answers—they have permission to show up as themselves in the learning process. Listening also helps us communicate to students that words matter. Making it a priority to listen to students alters the classroom dynamic so that learning becomes more like an active partnership rather than a passive exchange where we're the dispensers of knowledge and our students are the receivers.

Stay Curious Classroom Pause

Let's call this one the Stay Curious Classroom Pause. It's where we do more than wait for a beat before responding to what a student has shared with us. We go a step further in this scenario. We won't just pause, we'll let the student know that we're going to stop for a second to give meaningful consideration to what they've just shared in real time. Here's a quick example of how you might do this: *So let's stop and think about this.* Pause. *Ask a question that draws a direct connection between the feelings or opinion(s) the student has expressed and the material you're covering.* Pause again and listen to give the student the opportunity to respond. *Reflect what you hear back to them.* Pause again to give the student another opportunity to respond. The point of this? To give every student in the classroom the opportunity to stay curious and keep digging in. Pay attention to students' responses. If you sense that this conversation is beneficial to all involved and the student would like to keep going, then keep going. If you sense that the student might want some help or a bit more time to think, then open the conversation up to other students in the class. Keep listening. Keep engaging. Stay curious.

Encourage Students to Keep Thinking

The third tool is extremely simple but useful. End class by encouraging students to keep thinking about X (the challenging part of the conversation that was difficult to navigate). Ask them to come prepared to continue their conversation about X in the next class. Let them know that you're looking forward to hearing their perspective.

Feelings of frustration, sadness, disappointment, confusion, and even disillusionment are all emotions I've journeyed through with my students. I've also witnessed my students experience relief, connection, joy, excitement, intense curiosity, brilliant inquisition, and witty, hilarious, and incredibly engaging banter. All of it (within appropriate boundaries, i.e., Terms of Engagement) creates a dynamic classroom environment. More importantly, when students have permission to feel, they begin to ask difficult questions they often aren't able to ask anywhere else. Discipline, determination, self-regulation, healthy curiosity, bouncing back from self-pity or self-doubt, learning to listen while feeling strong emotions, understanding perspectives that are not your own, and cultivating the skill of learning to critically examine your own thoughts (without beating up on or undermining yourself) are all tools humans need to engage in conversations about race that generate belonging and connection instead of division.

 ## Make Tiny Tweaks

Release Perfection

I really struggled with this. Still do. I had such a clear picture in my mind of what my leadership in the classroom was supposed to look like that I felt wrong for making room for my students to feel. But I just couldn't escape the active engagement my students were showing me. It was too deeply connected to my primary goal of teaching students how to think for themselves for me to ignore. I didn't always hit the right balance. I certainly didn't always know what to do or say in the moment. But I was willing to connect, to meet my students where they were in their learning process. My students' feedback told me that it made more of a difference than I realized. So here's the thing: We don't need to be perfect, and we don't need our students to be perfect. But we do need to be willing to carve out space to feel so that we can engage in conversations about race in the classroom in ways that are productive and dominated by intentional choice instead of passive reaction. So give it a try. Start where you and your students are. Keep what supports student learning, and release the rest.

Connection Strategy 2

Read This If You Feel Completely Overwhelmed

This Is Tender Stuff

Navigating conversations about race can be a disempowering experience. We tend to avoid connecting with and listening to each other; we glance at each other and then reach for familiar conclusions. This is how we often approach conversations about race: see a person, judge a person, come to conclusions about a person, and then make it that person's responsibility to prove to us that they might be different from what we expect.

We haven't given ourselves (or each other) permission to express *feelings* in conversations about race as a culture. We have (limited) permission to talk about systemic inequity, discrimination, history, achievement gaps, political outcomes, current events, news headlines, social inequality, intersectionality, racism (in the abstract), pipelines, government decision-making, the policy implications associated with racism, implicit bias, and privilege. We do not have permission to talk about how race shapes the tender corners of our lives.

We all have feelings.

So instead of having conversations about race that connect the macro (systems, privilege, discrimination, history, etc.) with the personal (feeling forgotten, silenced, or being dismissed), we attempt to make ourselves heard by beating each other over the head with knowledge. This produces ever-escalating frustration. Since we all have feelings about race but we're refusing to carve out *space to openly talk with each other about our feelings*, our feelings explode into the big-picture, macro conversations we attempt to have. We sit down to talk about privilege, and in the middle of the conversation is a giant ball of pain.

We don't have permission to share our true feelings with each other. We do have permission to lecture at and attempt to fix one another. We keep having combatation, which makes sense given the cultural context we're operating in. It's difficult to have a real conversation about race when there's so much stuff clogging the pipelines.

Boundaries Are Really Important in Classroom Conversations About Race

Please hear me. Having boundaries in conversations about race in the classroom is not the same thing as protecting some students while attacking others or vice versa. Having boundaries in conversations about race in the classroom is not about helping some students realize that "they just need to do better" or judging and/dismissing unfamiliar cultural norms because you don't know how to relate. Having boundaries in conversations about race in the classroom isn't about fixing what some students think and validating what other students think because you happen to disagree (or agree) with their perspective. Having boundaries in conversations about race in the classroom doesn't mean handing some students a megaphone while silencing other students because you're feeling overwhelmed by guilt, shame, frustration, or the uncertainty of not knowing what to do next. Having boundaries while discussing race in the classroom does not require that you stake out a specific political position and then demand that every student who speaks align themselves with the position you've chosen. It also doesn't mean standing by as students personally attack each other; insult each other; use terminology that's deeply harmful, painful, dismissive, or offensive; or poke or prod each other (or you) in an attempt to provoke a reaction.

Crucial Tip
Choose to create connection.

The purpose of having boundaries in conversations about race in the classroom is to facilitate shared learning and discovery. That happens when we find conversation pathways that lead to connection instead of division (or avoidance).

This is literally the opposite of the way we talk about race as a culture.

Boundaries and Connection Don't Just Happen

Boundaries in classroom conversations about race don't just happen. Classroom conversations that create connection don't just happen. They will not (at least not at the time of printing of this book) be a natural outflow of the cultural status quo. It is highly unlikely that students will show up to class knowing how to engage in conversations about race that don't pit one person against another. It's also pretty improbable that they're going to walk in believing that they're entering a space where their point of view matters. It's even less likely that they're expecting a context where there is mutual respect and mutual dignity for every human being in the room.

Crucial Tip
We haven't figured out how to consistently connect in conversations about race as a culture.

It is far more likely that your students are anticipating that they're walking into an environment where their responsibilities are to (1) figure out what you think, (2) decide whether it's worth the risk to share what they think, and (3) keep what they think to themselves if it's not in line with your position.

This isn't connection. It's division. When our primary goal is to make sure students leave our classroom(s) thinking what we think (because we're convinced that the way we think is the only way to go), we'll never really learn what our students are thinking, we won't be able to facilitate classroom conversations about race that help our students connect with each other, and we won't discover the information we need from our students to help them learn to think for themselves. Making students think like we think is a different version of combatation. It's a barrier to learning.

It's also a barrier to our own development as educators. Navigating conversations about race in the classroom is a learned skill. We never arrive at the Nirvana of Classroom Education, where we've discovered all there is to be discovered about what it means to be a good teacher who facilitates optimal learning for students. This is an ongoing, unending process. We change. Our teaching style evolves. The tools we use shift, grow, and develop. Our needs change over time. Teaching that works is alive, vibrant, and vulnerable. It requires that we remain willing to take a look at ourselves and stay curious about how our teaching decisions impact us and our students. Teaching that works requires that we deal with our own stuff so we can create a space where students can release fear, connect, and learn.

Having Boundaries Isn't the Same Thing as Having All the Answers

Having boundaries isn't the same thing as having all the answers all the time. I'm still struggling to find the words to convey what I'm trying to express here. In place of the perfect metaphor to describe what creating and holding boundaries that facilitate classroom learning in conversations about race looks like, I'll offer you what I've got so far (ignore this if it doesn't resonate).

Boundaries help us make sure that the food doesn't fall off the kitchen table. We might turn over the plates. We might pick up a spoon instead of a fork. We might decide that we need a different tablecloth. We might open the blinds to let more light shine on the table. We might decide we need a break, and it's time to pull our chairs back from the table for a second. We might opt to serve unfamiliar food. Or perhaps it's an ice-cream-for-breakfast kind of day. (Yes, please.) But we're not having a food fight. No one's shoving fries up someone's nose. We may decide that we don't like how something tastes. Or someone around us might disagree with having ice cream first. We might move all the dishes all over the table. But the food is staying on the table. Nothing's getting shoved off the edges. And the things that aren't on the table are reserved for another meal. Or perhaps they're just so inedible that we know they'll be poisonous if we try to ingest them without help, so we bring in a chef who specializes in that item to help us navigate things safely. Everyone is free to come to the table. With all of their experiences. And they're also free to not come to the table. But the table is the place where we're going to engage. And the rules are clear. You don't have to engage, but if you do, engage in the ways you want other people to engage with you.

Crucial Tip
Engage in the ways you want other people to engage with you.

Let's Talk About Classroom Rules

I didn't have a ton of rules in my classrooms. But there were some nonnegotiable boundaries. Terms of Engagement that help keep us grounded and support our Foundational Goals are important (e.g., mutual dignity, mutual respect, listening, etc.). But there are moments when all of this can be a lot to remember.

I think that if I were forced to boil it all down, I would point to that last sentence in the previous section: *Engage in conversations about race in the ways you want people to engage with you.* This applies to every human in my classroom(s)—including me.

Navigating Potentially Disastrous Moments

I happen to be in a body of color. Society tells me that I'm black. That means that most of the difficult experiences I've navigated around racism are connected to being black: the insults I'm most aware of, the slights that bruise me most are all connected to being in a body that's primarily labeled black. I am much less familiar with the racism and other forms of bias that accompany belonging to any other racial or ethnic group. The pain I am most familiar with is the pain that is connected with the body I happen to have been born into. This presents me with many challenges when I'm leading classroom conversations about race, two of which include (1) I have huge areas where I can stumble with my words (note: my good intentions do not excuse pain that I may cause) and (2) the work entailed in educating myself on every single possibly racially offensive word I might use is so overwhelming that I can barely figure out where I would even begin.

Neither of these problems is unique to me. I'm hesitant to write this, but I think it's possible that to varying degrees, these are two pretty universal challenges for educators throughout our society when it comes to struggling through the race conversation. Let's take a look at the first challenge.

How to Avoid Stumbling Over Our Words
We tend to have the most transparent conversations about race with people who share our background or who are intimately familiar with our perspective: around the kitchen table, sitting in the dining room, riding in the car, sitting on the living room couch. Places that seem familiar, where we feel most confident we belong, are usually the places where we lean toward opening up and saying what we *really* think, where we're willing to say how we really feel. So when we sit to have conversations about race with people who have lived racial experiences that we're much less familiar with, it's not just that we're out of practice. It's that we've barely had any practice at all.

Then we enter into a more public setting, like a classroom, and we conclude that either we need to judge and fix unfamiliar perspectives, or we lean toward deciding that it's entirely pointless to attempt to engage in conversations about race at all.

When we're finished, we return to our relatively safe and comforting pockets to talk about our horrible combatations (and each other) using the language we're most familiar and comfortable with, all the while hurting (within ourselves and among each other) and wondering why it seems like "those people" just don't understand us. (This is problematic on so many levels, and I'd like to keep going, but it's outside of the scope of our conversation in this book.)

This complex challenge is (and has been) unfolding before us in live-time as a culture. It's a pressure that many educators experience. Something just feels off-kilter.

As educators leading productive classroom conversations about race, what on earth are we supposed to do about this?

Silence isn't really a viable option. Neither is pretending that we know all the words that are harmful, insulting, bigoted, or racist for every single people group within our culture.

My response to this question is not sophisticated.

We acknowledge our shortcomings, lead with listening, and ask wise questions, and take responsibility for our own learning.

I don't say this lightly. I ran face-first into this challenge while teaching courses I built from scratch focused on analyzing Supreme Court jurisprudence. Language norms have shifted over time, and there is case law with words now widely considered inappropriate, offensive, bigoted, and racist. Some phrases were flat-out appalling. But there were also words that I just wasn't sure about, terms I was simply unfamiliar with.

> **Crucial Tip**
> **Lead with listening.**

I struggled to figure out how to walk through this. But my students seemed to respond positively to a few strategies I used, so I'll share some of them with you here.

Avoiding Potentially Disastrous Moments Strategy 1

I explicitly acknowledged that there was offensive language present in the material we were covering. I emphasized the importance and value of respect and dignity and shared my decision to not use language I perceived as racially offensive—for anyone. That meant that even though students could read the offensive term (Supreme Court cases were assigned in advance of class and displayed on the projector at the front of the class), I would replace the offensive term with language that conveys dignity. That way we could look reality in the face (the words are printed on the page), and engage in dialogue while minimizing the chance of amplifying pain or causing harm in our classroom conversation.

Avoiding Potentially Disastrous Moments Strategy 2

During classroom conversations, I didn't facilitate an environment where students felt the need to tiptoe around their own words. I made the choice to model dignity, kindness, consideration, and respect for all people groups. Period.

Avoiding Potentially Disastrous Moments Strategy 3

I left room for feeling. My students were disturbed, and in some cases, shocked to read the dismissive, insulting, and condescending descriptive language used by the Supreme Court in past cases. Whenever this happened, I did my best to avoid letting my personal feelings about the content we were reading dominate the class discussion. Instead, I intentionally built in room for students to share how they felt about the material we were covering—all of my students.

This facilitated an environment where students could think about difficult and disturbing factual material without being put on the defensive or feeling pressured to become an explainer; neither of which is helpful in classroom conversations about race.

Avoiding Potentially Disastrous Moments Strategy 4

I took my responsibility to research and prepare for class seriously. Period. If we don't prepare, then it isn't fair to ask our students to trust us to lead vulnerable classroom conversations about race.

The point of these strategies isn't to help us feel like we have all the answers. By reaching for a guideline that supports my Foundational Goals, Essential Factors, and Terms of Engagement—engage in the way you want to be engaged with—I was able to facilitate an environment where we could have real conversations about race based on the material we were covering, conversations grounded in reality that avoid the pitfall of dismissing human stories and pain. These strategies invite engagement and personal responsibility and avoid creating a scenario in which we (educators) are expected to have the solutions for issues that we're still struggling to navigate as a culture.

Let's Talk About Fear for a Second

I can hear you. Pointing to newspaper headlines and saying, *Look, Krystle, I hear all of that, but I really don't want to end up in a national newspaper because I said something I shouldn't have.*

That's a valid fear. I've devoted a lot of time to thinking about this, and over time, I developed a general language boundary (let's it Good Sense Terminology) that helps guide my choices in the classroom with potentially offensive or explosive words and terms.

If I haven't suffered under the term, then I haven't earned the right to use the term.

And even then, let's be real, there are terms that I currently suffer under that I *still* don't use in the classroom.

Within our culture, we do great damage when we use words in ways that perpetuate the dismissal of human pain. This is not about people being touchy or quick to take offense. This is about creating classroom conversations that generate belonging and connection rather than division. Thinking that I'm using words that I know are harmful or offensive because I need to "toughen students up" or "prepare them for the real world" or "help them get over themselves" violates the boundaries I need to set (i.e., Terms of Engagement); disregards my Foundational Goals and Essential Factors; ignores my guideline for avoiding potentially disastrous moments (engage in the way I want to be engaged with); pits students against each other and myself; and points the classroom environment toward hostility instead of connection.

We don't always need to know exactly how to navigate problematic terminology, but we do need to be willing to be open with our students and hold ourselves to the boundaries we've set.

Now Let's Get Real About Not Knowing Where to Begin and Feeling Overwhelmed

The second challenge—"the work entailed in educating myself on every single possible racially offensive word I might use is so overwhelming that I can barely figure out where I would even begin" (see above)—is more about my own insecurities about leading classroom conversations about race than I care to admit. Here's why.

Expertise has nothing to do with knowing everything there is that a human could possibly know about each subject that a given profession touches on. Not one. (If you think of one, please tell me.) Being an extraordinary physician doesn't mean that you've memorized every possible disease and its potential derivatives (including the ones we haven't discovered yet) and can spout a lengthy list off within five seconds of listening to a patient present symptoms. Extraordinary physicians have cultivated the skill of staying curious, the art of listening, unrelenting determination, and carefully calculated persistence in the face of failure. Before I endured law school, somewhere deep inside I believed that my legal expertise would hinge on memorizing. But the law is extraordinarily broad. (In fact, there are so many specialty areas that [unless you were planning to go into intellectual property law] we were discouraged from over-specializing in our course selection.) Much of the expertise cultivated by attorneys occurs in the practice of law, which means that excellent lawyers don't have all the answers. Good lawyering doesn't begin with being a know-it-all; it's fueled by skilled listening. On and on, across professions, skill increases with engagement, listening, and proactive discovery. Practice. Exposure.

So why am I putting this unreasonable pressure on myself to know every single racially offensive word that's ever existed as an educator?

Because I'm afraid. I'm afraid of standing up there, in front of my classroom with my humanity on full display. As much as I want learning to be an interactive exchange, a partnership between my students and myself, the vulnerability involved is, quite frankly, petrifying. It feels like launching out into the deep, unsure whether I brought along the right oar.

The story that society taught me about what good leadership looks like is so different from what actual good leadership looks like in the classroom that I've learned that heading toward the feeling of being lost usually means I'm heading in the right direction: toward learning.

Navigating conversations about race in the classroom requires responsibly letting go of the myths of absolute control, having all of the answers, and the dream of arriving at the Nirvana of Classroom Education (where there are no interruptions, interpersonal dynamics to cope with, unexpected life changes outside of the classroom, administrative challenges, etc.). Doing the work of education in our society today requires that we be willing to show up.

And that's the scariest thing of all.

Crucial Tip
Show up as you.

So what did I do to counteract this pressure? At first, I overcompensated by working overtime to hide all my perceived insecurities (see Section II). That led to conversations that were stilted, awkward, and tense, far less productive than they could have been. But as I let go of the pressure, something shifted.

We started connecting as people. There was more space for shared feeling to emerge. Instead of the classroom revolving around my fear, we began revolving around the shared learning experience we were creating together as we moved through the material. Students and their learning moved to the center, and I continued to teach while learning more about how to facilitate their learning. As this shift happened, I recognized that telling myself I had to know each and every word that could possibly be offensive was a distraction from the work of proactively taking action so that I could learn how to responsibly lead the conversation.

If you, like me, have struggled with this fear, my response to you is to *gently move through your process*. Don't run from it. Through is the only way. I'm not telling you to throw good sense out of the window and get all willy-nilly with your words. But the one thing that you have that I never will is the ability to walk through learning how to navigate conversations in the classroom as you.

Remember This

When we show up to the conversation as ourselves, we're teaching our students the power of showing up as themselves. Slowly, we move away from posturing and the unnecessary pressure of putting on a performance. We begin to learn how to lead. We begin to move toward connection, discovery, healthy curiosity, and interactive learning.

This vulnerability isn't easy, but it's well worth it.

 Make Tiny Tweaks

When it's Just Not Working, Try This

In the moment when you realize that it's just not working, reach for conversation and connection—within yourself and then with your students. Ask your students what they're thinking, what they're feeling. Ask your students what they'd like to learn more about, whether they have any personal experiences connected to the material that they'd like to share. And then listen. Teach your students how to embrace the journey by releasing the pressure to know it all. Give yourself permission to show up right where you are, as you are, so that you can learn and grow together.

Connection Strategy 3

You Have This Choice to Make When Students Start Trusting You

What Happens When Students Feel Safe

Something was shifting. When I opened my mouth to speak, students were giving real consideration to my words. They were lifting their hands to ask hard questions of the material, of themselves, of myself, and of their classmates. They were willing to sit in silence and think before responding to questions from me or from each other. Dialogue *between* students was increasing, and I was shifting into a facilitator role more often. Students were taking ownership of the conversation. They were opening up, beginning to share deeper and more personal frustrations (we'll talk about Shared Story Blocks in Connection Strategy 5) in connection with the material we were covering, drawing from their life experiences and adding to the productivity of the classroom environment.

It seemed that the more I was willing to say,

I don't know the answer to that question, let me do some research and get back to you.

Or

Let me think about that for a moment. Pause, and then respond.

Or

Let's walk through this together. (And then wrestle with difficult questions.)

The more students were engaging, participating, speaking up, coming up to me after class to continue the conversation.

This caught me completely by surprise.

I knew that making connection a priority as we navigated classroom conversations about race was unusual. But trying something different (in an informed way within appropriate boundaries) felt like the only way to go if I wanted to generate real conversation. I was not at all, however, prepared for students to gravitate toward me. This was a risky choice on my part. I thought my approach would lead to me being considered, well, weird. Perhaps interesting on a good day. But that price was totally worth it if I could find a way to transform the race conversation in the classroom from combat into a connected learning experience.

There's a point to all this talk about weirdness.

There's an unexpected side effect to listening and showing up as yourself in the classroom.

When Students Start Trusting

Trust. Being safe to think, ask questions, practice healthy curiosity, and engage in real conversation about difficult things without being shamed, judged, condescended to, or being told what to think is refreshing and rare. It creates a sense of freedom, an invitation that transforms—one that nourishes growth and expansion instead of conformity to expectation. When combined with clear boundaries these experiences call us toward recognizing our capability, toward treating our own thoughts and discoveries with dignity and respect.

I've seen it start a ripple that grows into a wave in the classroom.

This trust looks like students being more willing to think aloud, students being willing to question not just what they say, but what I (the educator) say, what the course materials say, students drawing connections between the course materials, the content we're covering that day, and experiences they've lived. It's in the moment when a student voluntarily talks about what an alternative perspective to their own might be, and then begins examining why that perspective might be valid rather than dismissing it outright.

It's extraordinary to watch.

And terrifying. Because as students began to realize that I was committed to practicing and protecting boundaries for them, and not just demanding boundaries of them, *they began opening up and letting me in.*

> **Crucial Tip**
> When students feel safe they begin to pull back their Thought Curtains.

It's like watching someone pull back the curtains on their thoughts. The responsibility that comes with having this degree of access to another human being's development is gut-clenching.

The trust that students gave me meant that I had access to their thinking process, access to a deeper understanding of their strengths and weaknesses, a view of personal experiences that shaped their unique perspective, and, most terrifying of all, the ability to plant seeds and leave impressions about how they should or shouldn't think that would remain long after the class ended.

I could feel it. Hear it. See it.

I had a choice to make.

A choice that was completely up to me.

Making the Choice to Respect Students' Boundaries

Was I going to use my power as the leader in the classroom to manipulate my way into their thinking, reasoning, and decision-making, or was I going to leave what was happening behind the curtain alone because my students were entirely capable of thinking for themselves?

This is a layered choice—with significant ramifications. We won't unpack every single layer here, but I will share this core decision:

I chose not to reach in and mess around behind the curtain.

If I'm serious about not having all the answers, and about not expecting my students to have all the answers, then I have no business playing games with my students' thinking. I have no business sticking my hands into the incredibly vulnerable process students go through as they discover that they are entirely capable of thinking on their own. I have no business attempting to plant the seeds of the answers I think they should choose. *I have no business trying to make my students think like I think.* My responsibility as an educator is to teach students to think for themselves.

Students' trust in the classroom does not give us permission to start messing around with their thinking.

There's no reaching behind the curtain.

 Your Turn

Let's Explore Being in a Position of Power in the Classroom
*Grab something to write with and your **Brave Educator Action Pack** (get your free download at krystlecobran.com/the-brave-educator).*

Find a quiet spot and give yourself at least 15 minutes to work this exercise.

Think about this: You're in a position of power as the leader and facilitator of classroom conversations about race.

Write a few sentences (start with two or three) in response to each of the following questions:

1. How does it feel to think about being in a position of power in your classroom?
2. Are there any choices you want to make about what to do with that power?
3. Are there any personal boundaries you'd like to create for yourself (e.g., giving the respect that you want to be given, respecting students' ability to think for themselves, carving out space in your own life to process and think about race so that you make more conscious choices in the classroom, etc.)?

Write one word or a short phrase in response to the following question:

What do you want to do with the trust that students give you?

 Make Tiny Tweaks

You Are Not Forgotten

I see you. Getting up day after day, prioritizing your students' needs. I hear you. Asking questions that are hard to speak out loud. Wondering whether all the time and energy you're putting in is worth it. I know you're making the choice to be trustworthy even when you're not getting the support, feedback, or encouragement you need.

Your work is not in vain. Your effort is not pointless. Your service is valuable and important. And no one knows how to navigate your classroom like you do.

So take this content, and squeeze every drop of support, encouragement, and feedback out of it that you can. You are not forgotten.

Connection Strategy 4

Lists for When You're Worried Everything Will Go Wrong

Apparently, People Love Lists

I've been told that people love lists. I was unaware this was a thing, but I wrote this chapter in list format anyway. So if you happen to be an educator who loves lists, use these when things get tense, you're short on time and are wondering how to keep the conversation on track.

Crucial Tip
You can always change direction.

Avoid Defensiveness Trap

Don't get defensive because it does the following:

- ◆ Sucks the air out of the room
- ◆ Puts everyone on edge
- ◆ Builds barriers
- ◆ Messes with connection
- ◆ Sets up a "with me or against me" paradigm

- ◆ Gets in the way of learning
- ◆ Makes it harder than it already is to lead
- ◆ Interferes with trust
- ◆ Distracts us from the work of teaching

If you find yourself getting defensive, breathe deep. Set aside time to process your stuff. (It can be five minutes. Literally. Just start.) Because clearly, something is triggering you. Set a time and place outside of the classroom if at all possible. (I've found that commuting or taking a shower can be useful windows of time for processing.) It's not your students' job to take care of your emotions. That's your gig. So keep breathing. Your stuff belongs to you, your students' stuff belongs to your students, and you're the educator in the room. Press the reset button (e.g., *Well. That didn't go so well. Let's take a deep breath and try a different approach.* Then ask a new question to get the conversation moving again).

Keep Out of "I've Got a Point to Prove" Pit

Forget having a point to prove because it does the following:

- ◆ Makes the classroom a stage for your personal insecurities
- ◆ Shoves personal agendas into classroom conversations
- ◆ Teaches students to put ego ahead of learning
- ◆ Makes us talk *at* instead of *with*
- ◆ Messes with learning
- ◆ Sucks the air out of the room
- ◆ Creates distance instead of connection
- ◆ Gets in the way of curiosity
- ◆ Gets in the way of discovery
- ◆ Risks turning us into raving idiots

There is nothing more obnoxious than people who spend all their time with their mouths open and none of their time listening. Students don't respect or trust educators who are constantly trying to manipulate them into thinking what they think. It may be tempting to berate students into change, but the cost is high. Drilling down to prove your point is a really great strategy if you don't want your students to take anything you have to say to heart, which hopefully proves the point that proving a point doesn't prove a point. It proves fear and insecurity.

Stay Off of Taking Questions Personally Cliff

Don't take questions personally because:

- ◆ Discovery is pretty hard when students aren't asking questions
- ◆ Questions are usually a sign of learning
- ◆ Classroom learning isn't all about us and our stuff
- ◆ We're responsible for carving out spaces to deal with our own stuff
- ◆ Our students' stuff isn't about us
- ◆ We don't want to teach our students to reach for defensiveness in classroom conversations about race
- ◆ Questions help us understand the importance of context
- ◆ Everyone in the room brings their personal experiences to the race conversation, including you

If your students keep questions inside because they're afraid they'll offend you, you won't discover what you need to know so that you can teach them what they need to know. Questions (usually) lead the classroom toward shared discoveries. Listen and respond appropriately—within healthy boundaries, of course.

Avoid Validation Pit

Don't expect students to validate your personal perspective because:

- ◆ No two human experiences are utterly identical
- ◆ There is room in the race conversation for multiple perspectives

- ◆ Teaching and fixing aren't the same thing
- ◆ We're responsible for dealing with our own stuff
- ◆ Learning and resentment don't mix well
- ◆ Discovery isn't about you
- ◆ Our life experiences enrich the conversation, they don't *dictate* the conversation
- ◆ It's incredibly frustrating trying to control what people think

Your classroom is not your personal cauldron of validation. Remember your road map and the tools that best serve you and your students. Focus on your Foundational Goals. Point your energy toward what you really value, not toward all the ways you're afraid you're failing. *Use this book to fill your tank, and make it your priority to treat yourself with kindness.*

Avoid Unending Rage Trap

Whatever your political views are (yes, I said it), don't expect students to adopt your personal view on current events because:

- ◆ Boundaries are important
- ◆ Open conversation is better than hidden thoughts
- ◆ Learning and pretending to agree aren't the same thing
- ◆ Productive dialogue is better for learning than fake conformity
- ◆ Discovery is a journey, not a destination
- ◆ Sameness isn't necessary for connection
- ◆ Educators facilitate thinking, not parroting
- ◆ Your classroom goals are not dictated by current events
- ◆ Healthy boundaries leave room for multiple perspectives

This is a recipe for burnout. If you try to subsist off of pouring your energy into educating humans, being enraged, the preparation necessary for effective education, and the endless work that goes into being an educator, you're setting yourself up for extreme and escalating depletion. Please hear me. Feel what you feel. If you feel rage, feel rage. But if you let that feeling become the platform you try to educate from, you're going to get trapped. Your ability to be creative, flexible, responsive, present, attentive, and open will be directly impacted by whatever you're perpetually enraged by. And if you take your rage and try to funnel it into forcing your students to feel like you feel, you're going to break down whatever trust you've built in a fraction of the time it took you to create it.

Crucial Tip
Open conversation is better than hidden thoughts.

Stay Out of We Must Agree Before We Can Connect Pit (It's Bottomless)

Reject the premise that complete agreement is a necessary prerequisite to real conversation because:

- ◆ Conversations about race are enriched when there's room for multiple perspectives
- ◆ You're doing something courageous that we don't often practice in our society
- ◆ You're an educator, which means you're drawn to curiosity and inquiry
- ◆ You have power to create a classroom environment that incorporates myriad perspectives
- ◆ You've set aside defensiveness and aren't interested in controlling the dialogue
- ◆ You prioritize learning and connection
- ◆ You value listening
- ◆ You're committed to valuing both your and your students' perspectives
- ◆ You understand that the classroom isn't about your personal insecurities or validation

Mutual dignity and agreement aren't the same thing. Mutual respect and agreement aren't the same thing. Shared learning and agreement aren't the same thing. Shared discovery and agreement aren't the same thing. Remember your Foundational Goals, Essential Factors, and Terms of Engagement. Ask yourself, *Is complete agreement what I'm looking for or is there something I value more in this learning process?* Make choices that support your priorities.

Avoid Dismissing Surprising Thoughts Trap

Let students think their own thoughts because you:

- ◆ Choose learning over manipulating
- ◆ Refuse to believe that disagreement and learning are polar opposites
- ◆ Remember that classroom conversations about race aren't about what you think
- ◆ Remember that classroom conversations about race aren't about your stuff
- ◆ Resist the temptation to make students think what you think
- ◆ Respect your students
- ◆ Respect yourself
- ◆ Respect your teaching
- ◆ Are committed to the learning process

You are capable. Your students are capable. Make choices that nurture that capability.

 Share Your Story

I learnt a lot of this the hard way. Do you have any pitfall or trap stories you'd like to share with me? Visit krystlecobran.com/the-brave-educator and tell me about it.

Let's keep the list trend going, shall we? Here are four Tiny How-To Guides to help you through tense moments in the classroom.

Crucial Tip
We're all learning how to do what we do.

Tiny How-To Guide 1: Discussing Controversial Current Events in Class

How to navigate controversial current events:

- ◆ Identify the core takeaway you want students to walk away with. (It's useful to take a look at your classroom material and find at least one valuable concept that connects with the current event(s) you discuss.) Use that core takeaway to help students stay focused and connect the dots throughout the conversation.
- ◆ Listen. Always listen. And ask clarifying questions. (Don't worry; we'll talk about this in the next chapter.)
- ◆ In the middle of the conversation, ask, *"How does this connect to our discussions about _____ [insert reference to prior class discussion]?"*
- ◆ If you're ticked (and you have the time), let yourself vent before class. Call a friend you trust, journal, scream in your car (preferably in a private space so you don't look like you're starring in a horror film), or do whatever (healthy, safe thing) you need to do so that you don't dump your stuff on your students.

Tiny How-To Guide 2: Coping With Perspectives You Disagree With

How to avoid dismissing perspectives you don't agree with:

- ◆ Remember your boundaries. If you're committed to engaging with students in the ways you want students to engage with you, then dismissal isn't a great go-to.

- Listen. Ask yourself, *Is anyone being endangered? Is anyone being insulted? Is anyone's humanity being reduced? Is anyone being stereotyped?* If the answer to these questions is "no," then it's pretty likely that what's being said is triggering some personal stuff for you. And the classroom isn't the place to attempt to work out all your personal stuff.
- Remember to keep student learning at the center. Student learning is enhanced (note: don't forget your boundaries) when multiple perspectives are presented, not to mention that it's a better reflection of the reality of the world students are preparing to navigate.

Tiny How-To Guide 3: For When You're Tempted to Start Trying to Fix People

How to make sure you're not turning people into personal pet projects:

- Pay attention to your guilt. Notice when you start feeling badly either because you're having to watch a student struggle with something you've struggled with or because you're recognizing that students are battling challenges that you've never had to think about. The discomfort and pain of conversations about race can be so triggering that it hurts. That makes us want to skip the journey of discovery and go straight to fixing because we're convinced that we have to do something—now.
- But it's not your job to fix people. Including yourself. If your guilt starts to feel overwhelming, then that's a signal that you need to make room to deal with your stuff, not a sign that you need to double down, pick favorites, prove a point, or make sure you do your best to ensure that some students get ahead while largely ignoring others. (Quick tip: stay observant to when you're negatively judging or dismissing certain students. It's often a signal that something painful has been triggered for you.)
- When you're feeling particularly motivated to do something *now*, listen. Listen to what your students are

saying, listen to what they're asking for, listen to the course material they want to dive deeper into. Listen to what they're telling you they need. Listen, ask clarifying questions, and respond. Resist the urge to fix. Respond. And respond appropriately.

◆ Continue your own personal journey, and keep dealing with your own stuff.

◆ Don't make classroom choices out of guilt (see the earlier point). Respect your students' capability. Respect your students' choices. Remember you're the decision-maker.

◆ Ask for help. It's not unusual to feel overwhelmed when leading and teaching classroom conversations about race that work. You are not alone. I repeat: You are not alone.

◆ Take action from a place of intention, responsibility, and clarity; not guilt.

Tiny How-To Guide 4: When It Gets a Little Weird

How to navigate awkwardness when students say horribly offensive things (either because they just don't know or because it's what they think):

◆ Education is a layered process. So are conversations about race. Part of leading and facilitating effective classroom conversations about race is undeniably about building in room for awareness. Expanding awareness. Exposure and connection with unfamiliar stories. Because of our cultural context (see earlier conversations), there are situations where students may say things that are incredibly offensive because they are in the process of learning what they do not yet know.

◆ Respond; don't react. (Note: if a student is clearly attacking another student with insulting, demeaning, or offensive language, that's off the table. Hold the boundary.) But don't stop there.

◆ Engage, don't shame. Refuse to let your reaction control the direction of the classroom conversation. It may be difficult or uncomfortable. But it's part of education.

Respond in a way that increases awareness. Let students' stuff be their stuff. Engage in a way that helps students understand that they're responsible for the words that come out of their mouth. Listen, consciously respond, ask clarifying questions, direct students back to the material, and invite student engagement in ways that promote connection, conversation, and learning for every single student in the classroom.

◆ Prioritize safety. If something feels off, pay attention. I would be remiss if I didn't mention this at least once in a book that's about leading and facilitating classroom conversations about race that work within today's culture. Know your chain of command. Say something to an administrator. Again, respond; don't react.

 Make Tiny Tweaks

Unpredictable Doesn't Mean You're Failing

Conversations about race in the classroom can be challenging, and sometimes even blindsiding. The key to navigating this unpredictability isn't pretending, excessive pressure, or posturing. It's making the choice to *engage with what is*. Our students are telling us what they need. Our own questions are pointing us toward the tools and support we need. Remember: what we don't know helps guide us toward learning and discovery. Use the tips, road map, and tools throughout this book to create boundaries, shape your direction, and put supports in place so that your energy goes toward discovery and you aren't drained by fear and hesitation.

Connection Strategy 5

Try This When You're Not Sure What to Do Next

We all have moments in the classroom that catch us by surprise: moments when a student's response feels waaayyy off base, the path we created to gently guide students into productive dialogue seems to be leading somewhere entirely different, or we need to find a way to help students start the conversation (when we assumed that race was going to organically come up based on the course materials) and we have no idea what to do next.

If you find yourself in one of these moments, please know: I get it. Here are some options and strategies to help you feel more prepared to navigate those awkward situations when you're just not sure what to do next.

When a Student Says Something That Just Feels . . . Off

Something was off. We were slowly drifting toward quicksand. Our classroom conversation wasn't moving toward productivity, connection, or shared discovery. The way this student and I were communicating felt circular, not in the we're-on-an-educational-path-that-leads-to-discovery kind of way but in the frustrating I'm-not-sure-we're-having-this-conversation-on-the-same-planet kind of way. I could feel students in the class shutting down. The conversation was too detached from the focus, tone, and direction of our class. Every student contribution is important. But this particular contribution felt so ungrounded that instead of pushing the dialogue forward, it was like suddenly trying to veer down I-40 while moving up the on ramp for I-75.

I felt so torn. Student engagement and participation are deeply important to me. I definitely didn't want to shut down or shame this student into silence. But I also knew that I couldn't let this conversation-gone-awry shape the entirety of our classroom dialogue. It would leave us all feeling more confused than when we started.

I had no idea how to navigate this, but there were a few options at my fingertips. (Some more optimal than others.) Let's peek inside my brain and have a conversation about a few of them.

Option 1: Let's Ignore the Problem

Race is a topic so fraught with tension that ignoring the problem almost always seems like the most rational way to proceed. As educators we can get so consumed with appearing neutral that we lose track of the reality that conversations about race in the classroom have to be grounded in *something*. And that something needs to be something other than our personal discomfort with how the conversation has gone sideways.

One of the overarching guiding goals in my classrooms is helping students think for themselves. I'm not interested in students walking away from my classroom well-versed on what *I* think about the material we've covered. At all. In fact, I prefer for my students to literally have no idea about what my opinion is. I'm committed to facilitating a classroom environment where students actively discover how capable they are at thinking for themselves. I want them to wrestle with the material without using the trap doors of distraction or finger-pointing to move away from thinking and toward resting on preset assumptions. Ignoring the problem doesn't line up with this Foundational Goal. Instead, ignoring the problem puts my discomfort at the center of our classroom discussion. Not optimal. Next option.

Option 2: Let's Pretend That What This Student Is Saying Makes Sense

It can be profoundly uncomfortable to talk about race in the classroom. But we're doing it anyway. Great. Now here we are in this awkward dialogue, and this student had the courage to speak up and participate. I want to reward and encourage that engagement. The trouble is, what this student is bringing to the table is pulling us away from the content we need to focus on. If I follow this student down the trail without caution, then the entire class might follow *me* down a path that's completely unproductive (and potentially unsafe). So I can't pretend. That won't cut it. Which leaves me wondering, *How can I engage this student, keep the rest of the classroom engaged, and move us back toward covering the material?*

Option 3: Let's Get Critical, Critical

I could make this student's unexpected journey down a rabbit trail about me. I could take it personally. *How dare this student say these things after I've put all this time and energy into prepping classroom material that helps us have meaningful conversations about race? Doesn't this student understand how much work it takes for me to even stick my toe into this conversation? No one is paying me for this. Why should I have to navigate all the responsibilities on my plate and find a way to shape classroom conversations in ways that are productive when students are going to say stuff that's this off the wall? I'm tired. I want to go to bed.* You get my drift. When things go sideways in classroom conversations about race, it's easy for me to interpret it as some sort of personal attack, as an indication that my skills just aren't up to snuff, and I should just give up, keep things superficial, move through the material as quickly as possible, glaze over the difficult questions and get on with it. (Hey, it's not cute, but it's real.)

When I am calm and clear-headed and making decisions about how I want to show up in my classroom, this picture of Defensive Krystle (feel free to insert your name here if you relate) isn't who I want to be. (Deep breath.) I need to make conscious decisions about how I'm going to respond in this situation. So on top of figuring out how to maintain engagement and cover the material, I need to find a tool that helps me keep moving through teaching the material when I feel exhausted, overwhelmed, and frustrated. (Have mercy, this is so much work.)

This leads us to Option 4. Here are the tools I've found (so far) that seem to be useful in nearly every single sideways-drifting conversation about race that comes up in the classroom:

Option 4: Let's Listen (the First Tool)

The first thing I need to do when a student says something that's connected to our classroom dialogue about race but seems completely off the wall is listen. Listen. *Listen.* I need to hear the actual words that are coming out of students' mouths and avoid the trap of jumping to a conclusion based on the first three syllables I hear. More than once, a student has started saying something that felt like they were heading down a completely unproductive path and it turned into an incredible opportunity for the entire class (including me) to learn a new angle or perspective that was directly connected to the material we were covering. Just because a student starts saying something that I hadn't previously fathomed doesn't mean that what the student is sharing isn't actually a valuable contribution.

If my goal is to help students learn to think for themselves, then I need to be willing to support the process that creates that learning. I've got to be willing to listen.

 Your Turn

Let's Explore What Listening Looks Like in Your Classroom

*Grab something to write with and your **Brave Educator Action Pack** (available for free download at krystlecobran.com/the-brave-educator).*

Carve out 30 minutes to write your response to the following questions:

1. How do you feel about using listening to stay connected to students when things go haywire?

2. How would using listening and asking clarifying questions shift the dynamic in your classroom?
3. Knowing yourself and your students, what would this *look* like for you? (Be as concrete and specific as you can.)

Let's dig in, and come up with some options that fit you and your classroom:

◆ Does it mean pausing for five seconds every _____ [insert a number] minutes to take a deep breath and then ask a question (instead of lecturing)?
◆ Does it look like making a mental note to look up or turn around to make eye contact when students raise their hands to ask a question?
◆ How can you use listening and asking clarifying questions to support your specific classroom environment?

Come up with three ways you can implement more listening in your classroom and then give them a try. Use the space below (in your **Brave Educator Action Pack**) to notice how your choice to listen more affects your classroom.

Five Quick Benefits of Choosing to Listen When You're Not Sure What to Do Next

Listening Benefit 1

It helps every other student in the class understand that learning isn't about parroting back what they (students) think is happening in my (educator) brain. Real learning is not about pleasing me, validating me, or reinforcing my perspective or outlook. Learning is an interactive exercise that every person in the classroom is responsible for participating in shaping. Students need to know *I don't expect you to think like I think. Just think. Engage. Connect. Discover.*

Listening Benefit 2

Listening to our students helps us as educators understand where our coverage of the material is unclear. There are always places where students need to dig deeper or get a bit more support. Off-the-wall questions can be live-time feedback about what's clear, what's not, and where we need to try a different angle.

Listening Benefit 3

It gives us a moment to catch our breath. Conversations about race can get reactive fast. Part of our responsibility as educators is to regulate ourselves so that we can consciously respond to the needs our students share. Pausing, taking a breath, and giving ourselves a moment to reflect (i.e., *Let me think about that for a moment*) are tools that are easy to miss but vital in helping us respond instead of getting stuck in a Defensive Reaction Trap.

Listening Benefit 4

Students are always watching. There's always that student who's thinking brilliant things in their head but not saying anything aloud because they're afraid of not being perfect. Then there's the student who's a verbal processor, but they're wondering whether they should just keep their thoughts to themselves even though they learn best by talking out loud. Then there's the student who thinks everything through (and then thinks some more) before ever daring to speak a word. Plus an infinite variation in between.

Leading conversations about race in the classroom isn't the same thing as attempting to constantly control the conversation so that every student's contribution sounds like the conversation that is happening in our own head. When we listen *and then respond with a clarifying question*, our perspective, and the perspective of every student in the classroom grows just a little as we learn how to understand unfamiliar perspectives together.

Listening Benefit 5

When we practice listening, we discover where we need to adjust our approach so that classroom conversations can be more productive (this is connected to Listening Benefit 2). For example, let's say a student says something that feels incredibly off base (but not demeaning to other humans). When we start with listening, we'll learn (1) whether the student has misunderstood something about the material we're covering, (2) whether the student is confused about a piece of the content we're working through, (3) whether the student is struggling with something we've said, (4) whether the student is trying to connect the dots between the material we're covering and something another student has said, (5) whether the student is trying to figure out the deeper significance or relevance of content we're covering, (6) whether the student is attempting to distract themselves or other students from something that scares them or makes them uncomfortable, etc. . . . Once we have this information, we have the ability to respond to the actual need the student is sharing with us (and that other students who aren't speaking might have too) and reinforce healthy boundaries in ways that engage the entire classroom.

Option 4 (Continued): Ask Clarifying Questions (the Second Tool)

This simple tool can help us tackle the needs we detect once we start listening: Ask a clarifying question.

Asking clarifying questions will change your life. It certainly has changed mine. Here's how it works.

When a student says something that you don't understand, and you're attempting to find connections with the material you're covering ask a direct question (no passive-aggressive questions allowed) that directly communicates (1) you're listening, (2) you care, and (3) you're willing to help the student through the hard work of connecting the dots.

You are giving your students priceless gifts by practicing listening and then asking clarifying questions. You are:

Inviting connection
Communicating respect
Encouraging engagement
Teaching leadership

Demonstrating listening
Cultivating critical thinking
Facilitating student self-reflection
Stimulating productive dialogue
Discovering important details that will shape your teaching
Identifying areas where students need clarification
Learning how to lead conversations about race in your
    classroom that work for your students in live time

Your Turn

Scripts for Responding to Student Statements/ Questions That Catch You by Surprise

*Grab something to write with and your **Brave Educator Action Pack** (get your free download at krystlecobran.com/the-brave-educator).*

Let's create two Clarifying Question Scripts.

Clarifying Question Script 1

I think you're saying _____ [insert your understanding about what the student is saying here. Give the student a chance to pinpoint exactly what they're asking about.] Does that mean you're concerned about _____ and _____ [begin breaking things down and helping the student connect the dots]?

Clarifying Question Script 2

It takes a lot of courage to talk about _____ [insert topic student is asking about here]. I want to make sure I'm understanding you correctly. Are you saying _____ [insert your understanding about what the student is asking here]?

Now, let's take 10 minutes to identify two or three Short Clarifying Questions that can work for you in your classroom, with your students. Here are a few options to help you get started:

Do you mean _____?
Are you asking me _____?
Would you like to know _____?
Do you remember when we discussed _____ [previously covered topic] in our class about _____ [describe the past class here]? How can we use _____ [previously covered topic] to answer this question?
Is there another way we could approach _____?
Could you tell me more about _____?

Pick two or three that feel like a really good fit, and then write down on an index card you keep near your desk. Just as a simple reminder. If you find yourself caught completely off guard, breathe deep, practice listening, and reach for a clarifying question that keeps the class moving forward.

When we ask clarifying questions, we take the focus off our fear and worry about how to respond and put the focus back where it belongs: on student learning. Clarifying questions shift the dynamic of the room and put students at the center, giving them a sense of power, dignity, capability, and respect that fuels learning.

And if a student is just so completely off base that they're truly being ridiculous?

Then listening and asking a clarifying question gives students the space they need to recognize that they need to make a more conscious choice about how they want to show up in the classroom conversation. It's an invitation to our students to give themselves and the classroom exactly what we're giving to them. This approach invites each person in the classroom to discover the importance of listening and asking clarifying questions rather than resting on our own assumptions.

Listening and asking clarifying questions is a combination that points us toward shared learning, discovery, and connection and away from the potent quicksand of disconnection, defensiveness, and shame.

Your Turn

Listening and Asking Clarifying Questions
Begins With You

*Grab something to write with and your **Brave Educator Action Pack** (get your free download at krystlecobran.com/the-brave-educator).*

This is going to feel like a strange exercise. You're the person asking the questions and responding to the questions. But I'm asking you set aside 20 minutes to do it anyway. (If it ticks you off, send me a note at krystlecobran.com/the-brave-educator. We can laugh about it together.)

Step 1: Listen

I feel really uncomfortable when _____ [insert race-related topic here] comes up in classroom conversations about race.
Pause. Breathe. Listen to what you're thinking/saying. Write it down.

Step 2: Ask a Clarifying Question (or two if you find it helpful)

Do I feel uncomfortable because _____ [insert reason(s) you think you might be uncomfortable here]?
Do I wish I understood more about _____ [insert reason(s) you think you might be uncomfortable here]?
Do I wish I had more support around _____ [insert reason(s) you think you might be uncomfortable here]?
(Take your time. I'll wait for you.)

Now, what did you just learn about your needs that you didn't know before? *Write it down.*

Step 3: Take Action

What step are you going to take today to help yourself feel more supported as you navigate _____ [insert race-related topic here] during conversations about race in your classroom?

Here are a few examples of ways you can Make Tiny Tweaks:

Borrow a book exploring this topic from the library.

Listen to a podcast conversation about this topic during your commute.

Brainstorm your questions with a friend/colleague you trust.

Please note: The point of this question is not to beat up on yourself or shame yourself for what you don't know. It's to practice asking yourself questions that help you feel heard and supported.

Keep breathing deep. Keep practicing giving yourself the support you need. Be proactive and attentive to your needs. It will help you give the same support to your students.

Listening Is a Skill We Need to Teach

Standing in the classroom and actually listening to our students can be revolutionary. This is not an overstatement.

Crucial Tip
When we practice listening, we're teaching listening.

When we listen to our students, we're encouraging them to listen to themselves *and* each other. We're validating their capability, courage, engagement, and thought processes in ways that remain with them long after they've left our classrooms. When we practice listening, we're teaching listening.

What If You Need to Start the Conversation?

Not every conversation about race in your classroom will start *in response* to something a student says. There are times when your course materials, a class project, current events, or even a public holiday calls for a classroom conversation about race. I've included a *Get the Conversation Started Mini Road Map* that will help you if you feel stuck and need to get things rolling.

Share Your Story

Have you ever struggled to get the conversation started? Share your story with me at krystlecobran.com-the-brave-educator.

A Mini Road Map to Help You Get the Conversation Started

Here's a mini road map to support you in starting conversations in the classroom:

1. *Identify Your Foundational Goals.* Getting clear about what you value in the conversation will help you know how to guide the conversation. This might not seem like a big deal, but it is. Once you bring race up in your classroom, *you don't actually know how students are going to respond.* Your Foundational Goals will help you through so you don't slip into the traps of getting defensive or deflecting valid student questions simply because you're caught completely off guard.

2. *Identify Your Terms of Engagement.* Communicate them to your students (don't have an Inside My Brain Only conversation and then presume your students are thinking what you're thinking) before beginning the conversation. Remember, we haven't yet come to a broad, encompassing cultural agreement about how to have a real conversation (not combatation) about race. Your classroom may be the first place students have encountered genuine conversation about race. Take the time (before class) to identify two or three nonnegotiable Terms of Engagement, and commit to more than just communicating them to your students. Live them out with your choices as you teach.

Crucial Tip
Remember that you have the power
to set the tone.

3. Here are a few strategies to help you get the conversation moving in the classroom:

◆ Create Connection Springboards. Look at the classroom material you're covering that day, and take a few minutes before class to identify the content where race is most relevant. Find connections between the content you're covering and the conversation you want to start. Make a list of two or three questions to help your students explore the connections you've identified.

◆ Draw on current events. Pay attention to topics that really get your students' attention in class. Look at your syllabus/agenda/benchmarks. Are there any well-researched, fact-based articles directly connected to the material you're covering that would give your students the opportunity to think about concepts they're learning in new ways, or apply concepts they're familiar with in unfamiliar contexts?

◆ Share a personal story. Perhaps you heard a clip on National Public Radio (NPR), watched a documentary on Public Broadcasting Service (PBS) or saw a TED Talk that's directly connected to the course material and the conversation you're having that day. Consider sharing that content (in advance if possible), your response to it, and asking your students to join the conversation. It's a warm approach that invites your students to explore connections through down-to-earth conversation.

Crucial Tip
Use Shared Story Blocks to connect personal
stories with classroom material.

◆ Be strategic about the content you cover when you know conversations about race are coming up. Include content that gives your students the tools they'll need to have productive conversations when the time comes. Examples include reading books about the importance of listening, watching TED Talks that emphasize the value of understanding unfamiliar stories, teamwork exercises that help students grasp the power of words, class projects/assignments/books that help students understand the power of ideas and the importance of paying attention to our own thoughts and words, and building Shared Story Blocks—periods when students can share personal stories with you and their fellow students that are connected to/inspired by the course material—into your classes. Start with blocks of 5, 10, or 15 minutes. (If you notice that this really resonates with your students and promotes learning, you might consider designating entire class periods as Shared Story Blocks.) The perk of this approach? You're building time into class for students to learn how to productively have the race conversation and helping students learn how to make the course material their own (i.e., think for themselves) at the same time.

 Make Tiny Tweaks

Your Story Is Important

Don't forget our earlier conversations about how to use this book. Take what works for you and leave the rest. Adapt it. Mold it. Shape it to fit your unique classroom needs. I believe in your capability.

So ask difficult questions of this material. Pull the pieces you find most valuable, and start building on them. Pay attention to what you see happening in your classrooms, and *resist the urge to dismiss or downplay your discoveries*. Make adjustments, and keep tweaking. You are free to set the tone, shape the direction, and create productive classroom conversations about race that are grounded in shared conversation, learning, discovery, and connection. Keep listening. And when you just don't know what to do next, give yourself permission to keep learning how to do this.

Connection Strategy 6

Mini-Conversations for When Time Is Tight

Preparing for class can be time-consuming and exhausting. Educators juggle leading students through big-picture themes while helping them digest all the details they need to understand for course materials to make sense. There are so many moving pieces that it's easy to blow by things like staying curious and being conscious as we navigate it all.

Since you may be running low on time, I've created four mini-conversations to help you when you're struggling to select classroom materials, create interactive classroom exercises, respond to student questions, and get students to consistently speak up in the classroom.

Mini-Conversation 1

For When You're Picking Out Books (or Other Materials)
No one wants to feel forgotten. It hurts. Always ask yourself *Who's missing?* when you're picking out books or other reading material for your classrooms. Get curious. Start noticing things. Notice whether people in certain bodies are always

wearing particular clothes, have their hair styled a particular way, have a certain pattern of speech assigned to them,
are always standing on the side or are treated as comic relief.
Pay attention to who's the center of attention. Especially pay
attention to instances where essential pieces of human identity
are dismissed (e.g., accents, cultural food preferences, cultural
or religious clothing, family living arrangements, etc.). Notice
who is forced to justify their existence and who is respected.
Ask yourself if the way people are being treated in the material you're assigning lines up with your Foundational Goals,
Essential Factors, and Terms of Engagement. If it doesn't, and
you still choose to use this material, then consider using it
as a springboard for classroom conversations about how the
content impacts on the way we see each other, and to explore
changes students would make to the material to establish
mutual dignity and respect.

Crucial Tip
Refuse to dismiss another human's pain.

This is very important. Listen. Get curious about the voices that
may be missing from your classroom conversations. This is a
very, very fine thread. Please hear me: We're not assuming we
know what a student thinks based on what they look like. We're
not assuming we understand a student's suffering because of
what they look like. We're not dismissing the experiences of any
student because of what they look like. *This is not a box-checking
exercise.*

Ask yourself these questions: *Which voices have permission to
share their experiences in my classroom? Which voices are silent in my
classroom? Which voices aren't in the room?* If you start to notice
missing voices, keep that in mind as you're picking out books
and other reading materials.

If every book you pick out represents your voice, then voices
are missing. If every book you pick is in reaction to your pain
around recognizing that voices are missing, then carve out time
to deal with your stuff. You see where I'm going here. The point

is to stay curious and make intentional and proactive choices that expand learning and discovery in your classroom. Learning how to be conscious and aware of the books and reading material we put in front of our students helps us move toward unfamiliar stories, instead of away from them.

Crucial Tip
If all else fails, remember that conversations about race are often conversations about belonging. Choose to create belonging.

Mini-Conversation 2

Remember This During Interactive Exercises

Remember that your cultural experiences aren't the cultural experiences of every student in your classroom. Cultural difference is not the same as cultural inferiority. Presuming inferiority because of difference is problematic, deeply insensitive, and profoundly insulting. Different from you (or what you're familiar with) does not equal less than. So when you create an interactive exercise in your classroom, be conscious of how you respond to cultural differences. Invite students (and I mean every single student in the classroom) to establish shared ground rules for how the class wants this experience to go. Consider making the creation of mini Terms of Engagement part of your interactive classroom exercises. By inviting all of your students to help set up boundaries, you are creating a shared set of rules designed specifically for this interaction that (hopefully) lines up with your Foundational Goals.

Crucial Tip
Don't assume that unfamiliar means inferior.

Do not forget that we haven't yet established a shared set of rules as a culture around how to have conversations about race in ways that promote mutual dignity and respect. (There are days when it feels like the rules are changing moment to moment.) Keep in mind the reality that if you want a shared set of rules in your classroom, it is your responsibility to establish and maintain them. Draw on the resources throughout this book (especially the chapters in Section II) to create something that works for your students in your classroom. Stay proactive, keep listening, and keep tweaking.

Mini-Conversation 3

Never Forget This When You're Responding to Student Questions

I'm not big on telling anyone what to do. But sometimes when time is short, it's helpful to have a few do's and don'ts to hold onto.

Don't dismiss. Don't assume. Don't ridicule. Don't scoff. Feeling like crap isn't great for productivity. We shut down; we pretend; we get defensive; we draw back—none of which facilitates genuine classroom engagement.

Engage with what is presented within boundaries. Use Shared Story Blocks (periods specifically designated for students to share personal stories connected to the material) in your classroom. Respond to students in ways that build connection, not division.

Mini-Conversation 4

For When You're Worried About Getting Students to Participate

Connection is an invitation, not a demand. Let's repeat that. Connection is an invitation, not a demand. You can do what you can do. Identify your Foundational Goals, Essential Factors, and Terms of Engagement. Deal with your stuff, and get familiar with your students' stuff. Keep your tank fueled and manage tender things with care. Engage with what your students share, and demonstrate what mutual dignity and respect look like. Prepare for class to the best of your ability, listen, and ask clarifying questions to help students connect the dots.

Crucial Tip
Connection is an invitation, not a demand.

Be yourself. Invite connection by being who you are instead of who you think you're supposed to be. Remember that it takes time to build trust and that after it's built, it must be reinforced and maintained to prevent wear and tear.

Exercise care in leaving room for conversation, selecting course materials that are relevant and engaging, and equipping your students with the tools they need to ask challenging questions.

Keep inviting connection from your students. Keep connecting with yourself. (Don't forget to listen to your own thoughts.) In my experience, as students begin to accept our invitation to connect and discover that we're genuinely committed to listening and responding with dignity, interest, and curiosity, they inspire other students to join in and accept our invitation too.

But know this: If you demand connection, and then you withdraw and pitch a fit (or get sulky) when you don't get it, you will not find it.

 Make Tiny Tweaks

Embrace the Journey
Learning is a journey. Be kind to yourself as you take each step.

And if you have an especially hard day, find something hilarious (to listen to or watch) and laugh your face off. Remember that you're not alone. Then get curious. Give yourself permission to tweak. Make adjustments that work for you and your students.

Connection Strategy 7

Make Tiny Tweaks in Your Classroom

Two Questions We're Afraid to Ask Out Loud

There are questions we're afraid to ask out loud. We're just so afraid of saying the wrong thing that we remain silent. Let's talk about two tender (and common) questions we often hold inside.

Before we dive in, I want you to know that each time someone asks me one of these questions, I can sense how worried we are about being insensitive, uninformed, or hurtful. This worry can quickly escalate into a fear that silences us, that motivates us to avoid engaging in classroom conversations about race entirely. That doesn't help anyone. It gets in the way of student learning, and stops us from journeying through the organic process of learning how to effectively navigate conversations about race in the classroom. What helps is learning how to build the classroom conversation one step at a time. Instead of trying to fix problems (before they happen), begin to pay really close attention to what works, what doesn't, and make consistent shifts toward increasing the things that work and releasing the things that don't.

This is the power of choosing to Make Tiny Tweaks. This approach reduces our overwhelm, lowers the pressure, and helps us stay curious and engaged as we learn how to get out of our own way, stop tiptoeing, and start taking small, consistent steps toward creating a classroom environment where every student knows their perspective and experiences are valued. Let's explore the first question.

The "Please Justify Yourself and Everyone Who Looks Like You" Problem

Question 1: *How can I avoid pressuring students from minority (or marginalized) communities to speak on behalf of every human who looks like they do?*

Here are a few practical tips to remember:

- Don't stop the conversation and stare at minorities or people from marginalized communities when race comes up. Ever.
- Every student in your classroom likely identifies as belonging to one (or more) racial or ethnic groups. Every student. This includes students who do not identify as being from minority or marginalized communities. Race affects us all.
- When students from marginalized groups are singled out during conversations about race, we often ignore the pressure and pain that imposes. Pay attention to pain. Don't dismiss it.
- Students are capable. Let them choose whether or not to engage.
- Don't make broad generalized statements about what you think it means to be associated with a particular racial or ethnic group (e.g., statements like *"All _____ [insert racial identity] people are _____ [insert assumption about character here]."*).
- Don't rely on movies, media, or other pop culture references to provide an accurate perspective about what life experiences are for individual students in your

classroom. (Please don't do this.) Keep this in mind for students from every identity.

Crucial Tip
Every student has a story. Every student deserves respect. Begin with listening.

- Listen to how students talk about their own identity. (It belongs to them. Respect that.) Don't presume that you understand someone's cultural and/or racial identity because of how they look to you.
- Don't pander. Again, don't assume you know anything about students' perspective, their life experiences, or who they are because of what they look like. Invite connection. Create an environment where each person in the room can show up as themselves.
- Let students tell you who they are and what they think. Do not tell students who they are and what you think they should think based on your assumptions.
- I'm intentionally repeating myself. Remember that every single student in your classroom has a racial (and ethnic) identity. Refuse to fall into the trap of believing that only students from minority (or marginalized) communities experience race.
- Create connection and belonging. Using race to isolate students, mock, or dismiss their perspective doesn't create connection or belonging—it leads to division and isolation.
- If a student who is part of a minority (or marginalized) community speaks up, listen. If a student who isn't part of a minority (or marginalized) community speaks up, listen. Do not minimize, dismiss, or force students to justify what they've shared because it doesn't fit into your personal life experiences or perspective. This discourages genuine engagement. (Plus, it models that behavior for every student in the classroom.)

Share Your Story

Do you have more questions that you're afraid to ask out loud? Use the Connect With Me form at krystlecobran.com/the-brave-educator to share them with me.

When Things Get Uncomfortable

Question 2: *I'm worried things will get too uncomfortable in the classroom. Is there anything I can do?*

Here are a few tips for navigating awkward classroom moments:

◆ Acknowledge that you're uncomfortable. (Out loud.) Breathe deep.

◆ Don't assume your students are feeling exactly what you're feeling.

◆ When students share their discomfort, don't dismiss their feelings. Engage with your students. Meet them where they are.

◆ Make space for discomfort. Don't rush through it. Notice it. Get curious about it. Don't try to fix it. There are lessons in the discomfort we can't get to any other way. (Exception: discomfort that results because of inappropriate or unkind behavior.)

◆ Reach for unfamiliar stories and experiences.

◆ Being uncomfortable doesn't mean that we're incapable of having the race conversation. Sometimes, it means we're learning something new. Notice what's happening in your classroom more than you listen to your fear.

◆ Feel free to share this anecdote from me: I (Krystle) literally help people have conversations about race for a living. I am always uncomfortable when I'm having a conversation about race. Always. Not once have I had a conversation about race and thought, "Wow, that was like sipping an ice-cold glass of water at the beach." Not once. The truth is that *the more I actively participate in conversations about race, the more I'm able to notice my discomfort and not let it dictate how I respond.* The point: learning how to talk about race is a learned skill. We won't learn how to do this unless we practice.

Crucial Tip
We learn how to talk about race with each other
by talking about race with each other.

- Being uncomfortable isn't a sign of failure. It's often a signal that you're heading toward connection and discovery. (Please note: Discomfort combined with any hint that a human being is being dismissed, disregarded, or made to feel small in your classroom is a very different phenomenon that calls for the practice of healthy boundaries immediately. Pay attention.)
- Don't abandon your students because you feel uncomfortable. Stick with them, ask clarifying questions, and proactively listen. Be responsive.
- Join your students in the discomfort. Being comfortable isn't the goal of real conversations about race in the classroom; focus your energy on creating connection, discovery, and shared learning experiences.
- Do not prioritize the comfort of some students over others. I repeat: Do not prioritize the comfort of some students over others. Please do not confuse being uncomfortable with creating or facilitating a hostile environment for any student in your classroom. Again, discomfort that results from derogatory or dismissive behavior is not the same thing as discomfort that results from shared learning and discovery. Healthy boundaries lead to connection, not shame. Stay aware.
- Humor is a very useful tool. (Please note: This does not include dismissive or insulting humor.) Humor that comes from stating out loud what you're feeling or experiencing can be powerful and help break up the tension

in the room (e.g., "*Well, I feel uncomfortable. [Deep breath.] Welp, let's keep going.*").

◆ Letting things be heavy sometimes is important. Race is one of the few topics of conversation that hovers nearly everywhere we go in our culture. Yet (as we've discussed), we rarely have the race conversation in ways that generate connection and belonging. So when things get real in the classroom, they might also get heavy. That's real life. Let reality be what it is. Learning how to deal with reality is an essential part of navigating conversations about race in the classroom with integrity. Our job as educators isn't to make things cute or to glaze over the tough stuff. It's to help our students learn to think for themselves as we (hopefully) prepare our students for life. So if something's heavy, let it be heavy. Trust that you'll learn how to move through it together. We get good at what we practice. (Yes, I wrote that grammatically incorrect sentence.) Heaviness isn't a barrier to real conversation, connection, and learning; it's part of the journey. So don't let it intimidate you. Keep going.

 Make Tiny Tweaks

Keep Asking Questions

It takes guts to ask questions. I spent years (years) of my life thinking that I had to prove my intelligence by having all the answers. This approach to learning drained my energy and left me feeling alone and trapped. The value of a question is difficult to overstate. Asking questions leads us away from fear and toward discovery. So ask questions. Do it with wisdom. Start noticing when people reach for curiosity before they grab conclusions. Build relationships with people who understand that we don't have all the answers. Read books and articles, listen to talks, and watch clips from thinkers of many different perspectives to grow more informed. Pay attention to your choices. Notice the decisions that leave you feeling wide open instead of depleted and crunched in. And please, please, remember that we learn how to lead conversations about race in the classroom by leading conversations about race in the classroom. Not just by thinking about it. It really, truly is a learned skill. So leverage what you've already got—your skills of observation, communication, connection, and discovery—and bring them into the classroom with you. Notice what opens things up and what weighs things down. Stay curious. Make Tiny Tweaks. Keep asking questions.

Afterword

For When It Gets Tough

This Is a Beginning, Not an Ending

The Brave Educator is a beginning, not an ending. When we feel overwhelmed and stressed, it's easy to look down our noses at beginnings. We act like beginnings are standing in our way, blocking our path, wanting nothing more than to mess with us. We push toward "the important stuff," convinced that our effort is only worth it when we start by tackling complex realities that haunt us. Resist the urge to dismiss the process. Educators are teachers; humans whose specialty is making content accessible and digestible. Give yourself permission to start. Keep overwhelm low so you can stay engaged in the process of learning how to navigate conversations about race in your classroom.

Crucial Tip
Your beginnings add up to create your endings.

Forget About Having All the Answers

Giving ourselves permission to not know so we can start learning and discovering instead of judging and pretending isn't a waste of time; it's where the work actually is. It's really hard to teach our students how to get through challenging conversations and content if we're not willing to struggle through ourselves. Embrace the struggle. Don't judge it. Or run from it. Cherish your mistakes, your victories, and everything in between. All of it will help you create conversations about race that work in your classroom.

Embrace the Journey

Resist the pressure to leap from knowing we need to talk about race in the classroom to assuming we should already know how to make it happen. Instead, focus your energy on practicing the real-life tips and strategies you need to feel supported as you learn how to navigate conversations about race in the classroom.

Crucial Tip
Embrace the struggle as part of the journey.

This journey isn't perfect. It's not complete. We haven't covered every single possible challenge or scenario that might come up. We haven't said everything there is to be said, but we have had a conversation—a real conversation, one that starts with beginning with admitting that we don't have all the answers.

Not Knowing Is Where We All Begin

Not knowing isn't failure. So let's transform pretending we have all the answers into an invitation to move toward shared learning and discovery. Let's break down the challenge of navigating conversations about race in the classroom from one giant (and potentially overwhelming) mass into digestible and doable chunks. Let's learn how to Make Tiny Tweaks. Let's do it with clarity, connection, inspiration, honesty, and laughter that lightens your load.

Crucial Tip
Keep Making Tiny Tweaks.

When you feel overwhelmed, breathe deep. Stay curious. Stay open. Draw on your capability and resourcefulness and the tools in this book. *The Brave Educator* is less of a formula and more of a customizable toolbox. Use it in the way that best serves you and your students.

No Matter What, Give Yourself Permission to Keep Starting

Give yourself permission to keep starting. When things get knocked off track, start. When things are going well, start. When you're not sure what to do next, open *The Brave Educator*, find a tool that can help you move forward, and start again.

 Share Your Story

Head over to krystlecobran.com/the-brave-educator to download your free **Brave Educator Action Pack**. While you're there, fill out the Connect With Me form to share your questions with me.

 Make Tiny Tweaks

Keep Starting, Keep Beginning
The truth is that the beginning is everything. Keep starting, keep beginning, and together we'll find our way through.

Where to Find Me

Want to Talk With Me Face-to-Face?

Here's Where to Find Me (Free Download)

Want me to come to your school or organization? Go to krystlecobran.com/the-brave-educator to download your free **Brave Educator Action Pack**. While you're there, fill out the **Connect With Me** form. Tell me exactly what you need. I'm listening.

One last thing.

Thank you for being a Brave Educator.

Acknowledgments

Thank you to educators for sharing your stories with me. Your courage helps me speak. Your frustration, tears, and open-hearted determination to meet students where they are and create conversations that work is palpable.

Thank you to every single one of my students. Your challenging questions, wisdom, willingness to wrestle with difficult conversations, ability to communicate with passion and truth, and raw capability leaves me in awe. I am grateful for you. I believe in you. This book wouldn't exist without you.

Thank you to Lauren Davis, Emmalee Ortega, Heather Jarrow (who got my proposal into Lauren's hands), Jennifer Bonnar, and Brian Ellerbeck, whose kind response to a proposal from an unknown writer helped me keep going. Your patience, responsiveness, resourcefulness, and kindness helped bring this book to life.

Thank you to Sandra Bond of Bond Literary, who has become my friend.

Thank you to the women who surround me, lift me, and help me stumble forward as I question everything. In moments I'm not certain I can go on, you show up. You keep showing up. Your kindness is transforming me. You are more important than you know.

Thank you to my support team. The humans who refuse to budge. You are the gentle hands and determined hearts who see me as I am. I have no perfection to offer. Your love points me toward truth. You help keep me alive as I travel this journey. I am grateful beyond words.

Thank you to Sarah Neuburger, who created the illustrations in this book. I adore your lines, and I am grateful for you.

Thank you to the five humans who journey with me through the ups and downs of life. The way you love me is helping me become myself. When all else fails, I know we will find our way back to each other. Thank you for being my witnesses.